macroeconomics

London School of Economics handbooks in economic analysis

EDITOR: S.G.B. Henry *Lecturer in Economics, University College London*

macroeconomics

Morris Perlman

Lecturer in Economics, London School of Economics

Weidenfeld and Nicolson London

© 1974 Morris Perlman

0297766910

Weidenfeld and Nicolson
11 St. Johns' Hill,
London SW11 1XA

Printed in Great Britain by
REDWOOD BURN LIMITED
Trowbridge & Esher

1091556-7:

22.9.95

contents

foreword

In keeping with the other books in this series, this text is comparable with a course currently given at the L S E. In this case the course is that given by Dr Perlman to students in their final years of the B.Sc. programme in Economics. As with other books in this series, then, this one aims to provide a short modern approach to the subject, as would a lecture course for third-year undergraduates or preliminary-year graduates at the L S E. Also, though the book is self-contained, it links with other books in the series (e.g. Thomas's 'An Introduction to Statistical Analysis for Economists') which are also integral parts of the M.Sc. programme at the School.

There are already so many many books on intermediate macroeconomics that special reasons seem to be required to justify the appearance of yet another. In this case it is relatively easy to provide such special reasons, but two features of the book in particular deserve to be mentioned: its coverage and its individual approach to economic analysis.

First, regarding coverage, it is apparent that Dr Perlman deals with a wide range of important topics even though the book is relatively short. Thus, beginning from a small expenditure-model approach, an international sector and then a government sector are appended. This latter is particularly noteworthy, since a feature of texts at the intermediate level is their treatment of the government sector in the most cursory fashion. This text goes a long way in redressing the balance, paying careful attention to the introduction of the government accounts in the framework of an expenditure model, and conducting comparative static exercises subject to the constraints imposed by the government's overall budget decisions. Finally there is a perceptive introduction to the demand and supply of money, and their determinants.

But it is perhaps the second feature, that of its particular analytical slant, that most distinguishes this book from others in the same field. Dr Perlman avoids reliance on mechanical analysis using geometrical or algebraic formulation. Instead he concentrates on conveying an understanding of why and how the particular technical method employed succeeds (or possibly fails) in representing the assumed economic behaviour. Technique, in other words, is developed not as a substitute, but simply as a vehicle, for economic analysis.

S.G.B. Henry

preface

Macroeconomics often suffers from the mechanistic approach of moving curves around to find their intersection, or solving simultaneous equations, depending on whether one's taste is geometric or algebraic. This book is not entirely free from this problem. However, an attempt is made to convey some insight into what underlies those curves which are usually pushed around so blithely. An economy is a complex system for transmitting information among decision makers, and providing incentives to act on such information. It is important to understand that the curves we draw and move around represent assumptions about what information and incentives are important, and what sort of links exist in the system to transmit the relevant information. The main aim of this book is to convey such an understanding.

The material presented in a textbook represents a body of knowledge that one has acquired as a student from one's teachers, and as a teacher from one's colleagues (and sometimes even from one's students). Much of it seeps in as though by osmosis, except, of course, for the errors which by the usual convention are always one's own. This makes it very difficult to attribute sources and express appreciation to particular teachers, colleagues, or students. I must, however, express my great debt to Mr Kurt Klappholz who has read the whole manuscript in his usual thorough and perceptive way. His suggestions have made the book freer of error and more readable than it otherwise would have been.

The questions for each chapter, at the end of the book, should be considered as an integral part of the material presented in the chapter.

I am grateful to Brian Henry who read the manuscript and made many helpful comments, and to Mrs Nancy Bergh who typed the various drafts of the manuscript.

Morris Perlman

chapter 1
introduction

In 1932 twenty-three per cent of the labour force in the United Kingdom, and nearly 24 per cent of the labour force in the United States, were unemployed. In October 1923 the rate of inflation in Germany was $32 \cdot 5 \times 10^5$ per cent per *month;* soon afterwards the monetary system collapsed and people reverted to barter. In September 1967, after much speculation (in both senses of the word), Britain devalued the pound; nineteen months later, after a quiet weekend, France did the same with the franc. It is true that the above are dramatic examples of the phenomena we shall study in this book – they were chosen for exactly that reason – but the phenomena themselves, unemployment, inflation, and balance of payments problems, occur in milder forms all the time. The purpose of this book is to present a logical framework for the analysis of these phenomena. What determines the level of income and employment in an economy? What determines the price level? How are these related? What policies can be used to affect them and how do they work? These are the sorts of questions that the analytical framework presented here is meant to handle.

Real income, employment, the price level and the balance of payments are ultimately determined by the interaction of the decisions made by all individuals when solving the economic problems facing them; decisions about consumption and investment, decisions about the allocation of wealth among alternative assets, decisions about how much labour to hire and supply, and many others. Even though these decisions are interdependent, it is useful first to subdivide the economy into various sectors of decision-making in order to examine what forces operate in each sector taken by itself, before looking at the interdependence among the sectors. Following this idea we partition the economy into five sectors of decision-making. The goods sector (chapter 2), the money sector (chapter 3), the employment sector (chapter 5), the government sector (chapter 6), and the foreign sector (chapter 7).

The goods sector is that sector in which we examine the decisions relating to the flow of goods and services. Over any period of time, a week, a month, or a year, an economy produces a certain quantity of goods and services – motorcars, symphony concerts, haircuts, and so on. This is a flow magnitude, ie it has a time dimension and is expressed as so many units of goods and services per some time period. These goods and services can be used for various purposes. They can be used to satisfy the current wants of individuals (consumption), or to increase the potential to satisfy future wants (investment), or for example to satisfy the wants of individuals in other economies (exports). The total quantity of goods and services produced in an economy over some time period, its total output, is also the real income of that economy for that time period. The latter is nothing more than the claims to the total output of an economy by the owners of all the factors of production used in the production of output; the sum of all these claims is equal to total output.[1] Of course, because of the cumbersomeness and difficulties of comparisons over time, of measuring real income as being so many automobiles, plus so many symphony concerts, plus so many haircuts, and so on, prices are used to convert all the goods and services into money terms, and these are added up to express real income as being so many pounds or dollars per period of time. However, it is important to remember that this is done because of the convenience of measurement and expression. What we are ultimately interested in when discussing real income is the quantity of real goods and services.

The questions we want to answer about the goods sector are what determines how much goods and services people demand during some time period? How are these decisions related to, and what is their effect on, how much is being produced during that time period? And ultimately what are the factors determining the total output and therefore real income of an economy? This last question will not be answered until we examine the output and employment sector.

The money sector is in many ways a misnomer, and should be called the wealth sector. In addition to the decisions about how to allocate the flow of goods and services being produced over some period of time, individuals have to make decisions concerning the allocation of wealth among the various assets in which it can be held. At every point of time every economy has a stock of wealth which is the sum of the accumulated savings from the past; in other words the result of past decisions not to consume. This wealth is held by individuals in the form of different assets. How wealth is allocated among assets, and what variables determine this allocation, is another aspect of economic decision-making we shall look at in order to determine how these decisions are related to those economic variables in which we are ultimately interested.

The employment and output sector is the one involving those decisions that determine the level of employment in an economy, and the relationship between these and the level of output (and of course real income). Here we close the gap left in studying the goods sector with respect to the factors determining the quantity of goods and services actually produced by an economy.

In the government sector we examine how government decisions can affect the economy, and in the international sector we incorporate international transactions into the model of the economy.

---

[1] Real income is measured by the real value of all factor payments (including profits). These represent the claims on total output by their recipients.

The rest of this introduction gives a brief outline of the method of analysis and general approach used throughout the book when examining the various sectors of decision-making and their interaction; what are the questions we ask, and more important why we are interested in the answers.

The value of any economic variable, whether it be real income, employment, the price level or the price of shoes, depends on the interaction among the economic decisions taken by many individuals or groups in an economy. These decisions depend on the goals of the participants — what it is they *want* to do — and the constraints facing them — what it is they *can* do. One of the questions we shall ask about the value of any variable we consider is whether it is an equilibrium value, ie whether the part-icular value is consistent with equilibrium in the market or sector of decision-making under discussion. By equilibrium we mean a situation which once attained by an individual, market, sector, or economy, will be maintained as long as there are no changes in the behavioural goals or tastes of the participants in the market, sector or economy, or in any of the constraints facing them. Equilibrium for an individual making an economic decision is a situation where he is doing what he wants to do *given* the constraints facing him. As soon as more than one participant is involved in determining the outcome of any variable it is not enough that each should be in equilibrium separately, ie that given his particular goals and his constraints, he should be content to continue his actions, it is also necessary that all participants are in equilibrium, ie that the equilibrium be consistent for all. For example, a group of buyers might be perfectly satisfied to buy *x* pairs of shoes per week at a price of £*y* per pair, given their tastes and the constraints as they see them; if at the same time the sellers, given their goals and their constraints, are only willing to sell *x* - 1 pairs per week at that price, both cannot be in equilibrium. Because the decisions of some participants (the buyers) cannot be realized, something will have to change (from price theory we know that under many conditions what will change in our example is the price of shoes). If, however, at a price of £*y* per pair buyers want to buy *x* pairs of shoes and sellers want to sell *x* pairs of shoes the decisions of both can be realized. There is no tendency for anything to change. All participants in this particular market are doing what they want to do given their tastes and constraints.

One of the first steps in studying a particular sector of decision-making will be to define the conditions for equilibrium in that sector. In other words, when and why do we think that a particular sector, given the behaviour and constraints involved, will be in a position from which there is no tendency to change? Of course, implicit or explicit in our conditions for equilibrium is some specification of the forces generated by the system in a disequilibrium situation and, if these forces are to bring the system back to equilibrium, we must have some hypothesis about the reactions of the various part-icipants in such a situation. For example, in microeconomics we define equilibrium in a commodity market as a situation in which the price of the commodity is such that the quantity demanded is equal to the quantity supplied, because at a higher price there will be excess supply and ultimately the *price will fall,* and at a lower price there will be an excess demand and ultimately the *price will rise.* The two phrases stressed contain the specification of what ultimately happens in this particular system in a disequilibrium situation, and simultaneously the explanation of how equilibrium (if it exists) will be achieved. However, this explanation depends on a behavioural hypothesis, because it is only via some such hypothesis that we can connect the variable affected by the disequilibrium situation (in our example the price of the commodity) to the actions of the individuals involved. It is only because we assume (or deduce) that the quantity of a commodity demanded or supplied depends on the price of the commodity that we can say that the change in the price will tend to bring the market back to equilibrium. Had we assumed that neither the quantity demanded nor the quantity supplied depended on the price of the commodity, there would be no link between the force generated in disequilibrium (the change in price) and the actions of the individuals involved (the demanders and suppliers of the commodity), and therefore this force could not act as a means of solving the disequilibrium.

Our approach in analyzing the macroeconomic questions will follow the pattern outlined above. With each sector we shall first ask what are the conditions for equilibrium in that sector and why a particular definition of equilibrium is sensible or useful. We shall then postulate some simple hypotheses about the behaviour of the various decision-makers in that sector and examine the constraints involved, to determine how equilibrium is achieved. We then consider what factors will lead to changes in equilibrium and how these changes will react on the decisions of the groups involved. We shall first do this for each sector separately and then put them all together and ask the same sort of questions about the economy as a whole.

It is appropriate to finish this introduction with a word of caution. The questions with which we are concerned are quite complex. They involve every individual making any economic decision. In studying the behaviour of the participants in the economy we shall make many simplifying hypotheses. However, it should be remembered, especially when the urge becomes strong to reject a concept because the behavioural hypotheses used to illustrate it seem too simple-minded (especially in relation to our preconceptions about the complexity of the 'real' world), that the function of analysis is not only (and sometimes not at all) to present a particular hypothesis about the behaviour of a particular group; it is also to learn a method of approaching various problems, tracing the interrelations involved and examining the consequences of various hypotheses about behaviour. The framework of analysis presented can be modified and used to analyze the consequences of more complex hypotheses about behaviour than those used to illustrate the method of analysis.

A related warning, at the other extreme, concerns the techniques we shall use. It is very useful to use simple algebraic expressions and geometric representations of many of the ideas we shall discuss. Most of these techniques are very simple in terms of their mathematical content. It should be remembered, however, that we are studying economics, not arithmetic. The use of an algebraic expression, or a curve, as a summary of some economic idea, relationship or interrelationship, might make it a very useful tool of analysis or aid to memory; it definitely does not make it a substitute for the understanding of the economic concept that it represents.

chapter 2

the goods sector

In the last chapter we defined the goods sector as that sector of the economy in which decisions about the flow of goods and services per period of time are made — how much is produced, how the goods and services are used, and how these decisions interact. To be able to concentrate on the 'demand' side of the goods sector we shall first make a simplifying but crucial assumption about what determines how much goods and services are produced. We assume for the moment that any quantity demanded *can* and *will* be produced. This implies that there are unemployed resources in the economy that can be used to produce more output whenever it is demanded. We also ignore the question of the mechanism by which an increased demand for goods and services will be translated into an actual increase in output. We shall examine these two points in greater detail when we analyze the output and employment sector. Following the programme outlined in the introduction we first examine what is the condition for equilibrium in the goods sector (section 2.1). We then look at the concept of the multiplier (section 2.2). We go on to examine some simple assumptions about the determinants of consumption and investment (sections 2.3 and 2.4), and then re-examine the equilibrium condition in the light of these assumptions (section 2.5). We finish with a brief examination of the effects of changes in the price level on equilibrium in the goods sector (section 2.6).

2.1 Equilibrium condition

We defined equilibrium as a situation which, if attained, would be maintained; a situation in which, given the behavioural goals of the participants in the particular economic process under discussion and the constraints as *they* see them within which decisions have to be made, nobody wants to change their actions and therefore there is no tendency for the outcome to change.[1] It seems sensible to define the

---

[1] The stress on the word 'they' in this sentence is important. The constraints as seen by individual participants, which are the ones that affect their decisions, are not necessarily the same as the constraints facing the economy as seen by an economist, for example. Thus even though we are talking about a less than full employment economy, one that is still within its resource constraint and therefore able to 'acquire' more goods and services, it may still be true that the constraints as seen by the individual decision-makers have already been reached.

condition for equilibrium in the goods sector as the situation in which the users of goods and services, given their goals and constraints, as seen by them, *want* to use up (for whatever purpose) exactly the quantity of goods and services actually being produced. For example, a simple economy which produces a hundred bushels of wheat per year will be in equilibrium only if people also want to use a hundred bushels of wheat per year. It does not matter whether they want the wheat to satisfy current wants (consumption) or to plant it to increase the potential for satisfying future wants (investment) or for that matter because they want to send it abroad to satisfy the wants of individuals in another economy (exports).

It is important to understand why any situation other than the one described above is not compatible with equilibrium (or why our definition of equilibrium is useful) and what assumption we are making about the reaction of our system to a disequilibrium situation. In our example, if people wanted to use only 90 bushels of wheat per year when 100 bushels were being produced, then literally there would be 10 bushels of wheat per year floating around in the economy which nobody wanted (given the variables — tastes or goals, and constraints — determining their actions). If on the other hand people wanted to use 110 bushels of wheat per year when 100 bushels were being produced, they could not do so, but their attempts to get 110 bushels will presumably lead to some sort of forces being set up in the economy — something will have to change. In both cases the disequilibrium situation can be eliminated either if output changes or if people's demand for output changes, or a combination of the two. Output can change if the disequilibrium situation (the 'excess demand' or 'excess supply' of output) affects any of the variables determining how much output producers are willing to produce, and so results in their changing their output. The amount of output that people demand can change if the disequilibrium situation leads to a change in any of the variables determining how much output people demand. For the moment we shall continue with the highly unsatisfactory assumption made in the first paragraph of this chapter and *assume* that a disequilibrium situation of the type described above will result in a change in output. It will be recalled that this assumption implies the existence of unemployed resources in the economy (otherwise output cannot increase) and ignores the whole question of via what mechanism the disequilibrium situation is translated into a change in output. If no mechanism exists then even if output *can* change from the point of view of the constraints facing the economy it *will not* change because of the lack of a signalling device and incentive to induce producers to change their behaviour. With these assumptions our previous disequilibrium situation will result in an increase in output to 110 bushels of wheat per year when there is an excess demand and a decrease in output to 90 bushels per year when there is an excess supply.

In our above discussion of equilibrium we have not mentioned prices. The equilibrium condition in the goods sector was specified in terms of the quantity of output and the quantity of goods demanded, and the assumed force generated in a disequilibrium situation was also in terms of changes in quantities. It may be appropriate to point out at this stage why we do not make the assumption, usual in price theory, that an excess demand or supply in a market for some good leads to a change in the price of the good which may result in the market achieving equilibrium. A change in the price of one good relative to that of another might lead to a change in the quantity demanded or supplied of that good (ie a change in the actions of the decision-makers involved). But here we are talking about all of output. If all prices change it is not obvious that anything real in the economy has changed, and therefore that any action by any decision-maker will change. If prices of output *relative* to the prices of factors change then there might be some real effects. However, before we are able to examine the effect of such a relative price change we have to study the employment sector, ie the market for factors of production. That is the main reason why at this stage we have made the unsatisfactory assumption about the behaviour of output, namely, that it will always change if it is not equal to the quantity demanded.

If we let Y represent the total quantity of goods and services produced by an economy per some time period (and therefore also its real income), and E the total desired expenditures for whatever purpose by all groups in the economy, then our condition for the goods sector to be in equilibrium is:

$$Y = E. \tag{2.1.1}$$

We also assume that in a disequilibrium situation whether $Y > E$ or $Y < E$, Y will change until a new equilibrium is reached.

To be able to say anything more about the goods sector (and so far we have said very little) we must analyze what determines desired expenditures. Total desired expenditures is too large an aggregate to handle usefully. We want to break it up into smaller categories that are easier to analyze. We have complete freedom of choice as to how to break up total desired expenditures for the purpose of analysis. Exactly how we do this depends on how useful a particular subdivision will be for the purpose of answering the questions we want to ask. One method might be to treat as a single category all the expenditures that are determined by the same economic variables; for example, to combine all the expenditures affected by real income in one category, all those affected by the rate of interest in another, and so on. Another method of breaking up total desired expenditures might be to do so according to the various decision groups making the particular expenditures, for example households, firms, government or foreigners. A third method might be to subdivide total desired expenditures according to the different purposes for which they are made irrespective of who it is who makes the decision or what variables affect the decision. For example, we could subdivide total desired expenditures into those made to satisfy current wants (consumption) and those made to increase the potential of the economy to satisfy future wants (investment). There are many other 'rules' that can be used to disaggregate total desired expenditures, and many degrees of refinement to which the disaggregation process could be taken. We can also see that many of the 'rules' overlap with respect to the categories into which various expenditures would be included. It should be clear that our definition of equilibrium in the goods sector, ie $Y = E$ holds, however we subdivide E, as long as the subdivisions contain all desired expenditures.

2.2   The multiplier

One important and useful subdivision of total desired expenditures arises from the dual nature of Y which represents both the total output of the economy — the quantity of goods and services available to the economy over some time period — and the real income of all individuals and groups making decisions about desired expenditures. If desired expenditures are behaviourally related to real income, ie if a change in real income leads to a change in desired expenditures, then there is a two-way relationship between output and desired expenditures. First, the relationship arising from our assumption about what happens in a disequilibrium situation, namely that if desired expenditures are not equal to output, output will change. Second, that a change in output, which is also a change in real income, will itself lead to a change in desired expenditures. The interrelationship between desired expenditures and the level of output which arises from our condition for equilibrium in the goods sector, *and* the assumption that desired expenditures depend on real income, can be illustrated with various techniques. We shall do it first algebraically and then geometrically.

Let us assume that desired expenditures consist both of expenditures whose amount is independent of income (E_o) and those whose amount depends on income (E_y).

Thus $E = E_o + E_y$. $\hspace{6cm}$ (2.2.1)

Let us also assume that

$E_y = \alpha Y.$ $\hspace{6cm}$ (2.2.2)

Equation (2.2.2) shows a particular behavioural relationship between real income and those expenditures which are dependent on real income.

Thus $E = E_o + \alpha Y.$ $\hspace{6cm}$ (2.2.3)

Our equilibrium condition is independent of whether desired expenditures are a function of income or not and is

$Y = E.$ $\hspace{6cm}$ (2.2.4)

Substituting (2.2.3) into (2.2.4) the equilibrium condition becomes

$$Y = E_o + \alpha Y. \tag{2.2.5}$$

Now assume that we start at some particular level of output, say Y_A, and that at this level of output the goods sector is in equilibrium, ie equation (2.2.5) above is satisfied therefore

$$Y_A = E_o + \alpha Y_A. \tag{2.2.6}$$

Now let us assume for some reason that desired expenditures change by ΔE so that at the level of output at which the goods sector was in equilibrium before (shown by equation (2.2.6) we now have

$$Y_A < E_o + \Delta E + \alpha Y_A, \tag{2.2.7}$$

and there is now an excess of desired expenditures over actual output shown by the second term on the right-hand side of (2.2.7). On our assumptions about the reaction of output to a disequilibrium situation, output will now increase by the amount of the increased desired expenditures. However, this will still be a disequilibrium situation because

$$Y_A + \Delta E < E_o + \Delta E + \alpha Y_A + \alpha\Delta E. \tag{2.2.8}$$

The last term added to the right hand side of (2.2.8) is the change in desired expenditures induced by the change in output (real income) of ΔE which was brought about by the initial change in desired expenditures of ΔE. Therefore there is still an excess of desired expenditures over actual output of $\alpha\Delta E$. On our assumptions output will again change by the change in desired expenditures. However, this is still not an equilibrium situation because

$$Y_A + \Delta E + \alpha\Delta E < E_o + \Delta E + \alpha Y_A + \alpha\Delta E + \alpha(\alpha\Delta E), \tag{2.2.9}$$

where the last term on the right-hand side of (2.2.9) is again the induced effect on desired expenditures of the change in output, in this case of $\alpha\Delta E$. This process continues until a new equilibrium is reached. The total change in output and real income is the sum of all the terms, except the first, on the left-hand side of an equation like (2.2.9) above expanded to include all the terms in the process described above. Thus

$$\Delta Y = \Delta E + \alpha\Delta E + \alpha^2 \Delta E + \alpha^3 \Delta E \ldots. \tag{2.2.10}$$

$$= \Delta E \ (1+\alpha+\alpha^2+\alpha^3 \ \ldots \ ). \qquad\qquad (2.2.11)$$

The terms inside the brackets form a geometric progression. If we assume that $\alpha < 1$ (ie that the change in desired expenditures induced by a change in income is less than the change in income) the sum of the terms in the brackets is equal to $\dfrac{1}{1-\alpha}$.

Hence

$$\Delta Y = \Delta E \cdot \ \frac{1}{1-\alpha} \cdot {}^1 \qquad\qquad (2.2.12)$$

Equation (2.2.12) tells us what the total change in output will be if expenditures change by ΔE taking into account the induced effects on desired expenditure of the change in output. $\dfrac{1}{1-\alpha}$ is called the multiplier and its value depends on α which measures the behavioural relationship between the change in desired expenditures and the change in real income.

The above relationships are illustrated in figure 2.2.1.

In this figure we measure total output per unit time on the horizontal axis; total desired expenditures per unit time on the vertical axis. The $45°$ line represents the equilibrium condition $Y = E$, and only points along this line satisfy that condition. Any point above that line would represent a situation in which $Y < E$, any point below the line one in which $Y > E$; both of which are disequilibrium situations. The curve marked $E_0 + \alpha Y$ is a representation of our behavioural assumption about the relationship between desired expenditures and real income. It should be clear just from

---

[1] This can also be seen in the following way. In the initial situation of equilibrium

$Y_A = E_O + \alpha Y_A$ (equation (2.2.6) above)

in the new equilibrium situation assume income is Y_B

$\therefore Y_B = E_O + \Delta E + \alpha Y_B$

the change in income ΔY is the second equation minus the first

$\therefore \Delta Y = \Delta E + \alpha \Delta Y$

$\therefore \Delta Y \ (1 - \alpha) = \Delta E$

$\therefore \Delta Y = \Delta E \cdot \dfrac{1}{1-\alpha} \cdot$

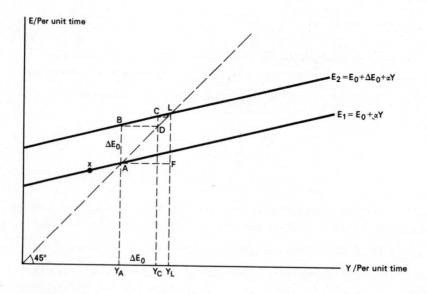

Figure 2.2.1

looking at the figure that this curve represents a relationship between desired expenditures and real income, not a relationship between actual expenditures and real income. A point like X (or any point to the left of A) is economically impossible in a closed economy. For example, people cannot use 10 pairs of shoes when an economy is producing only 5 pairs. However, they can demand 10 pairs irrespective of the quantity actually being produced. With the particular expenditure relationship shown in the graph the goods sector is in equilibrium at the point A because only at that point is it true that $Y_A = E_o + \alpha Y_A$, ie that desired expenditures are equal to total output. Now we have a change in desired expenditures represented by the new expenditure curve $E_o + \Delta E_o + \alpha Y$, ie a change of ΔE_o in desired expenditures. At the output level Y_A desired expenditures are now shown by the point B, this is greater than total output Y_A, and therefore actual expenditures cannot be at B. With our assumptions about the reaction of output to a change in desired expenditures, output will now change by $\Delta E_o = BD$. However, at the output level $Y_C = Y_A + \Delta E_o$ desired expenditures rise again by $\alpha \Delta E_o = DC$. The initial change in expenditures was a shift of the expenditure curve, from then on expenditures change because of a movement along the new curve induced by the change in real income. This process continues until a new point like L is reached where an equilibrium again prevails because at L it is again true that

$$Y_L = E_o + \Delta E_o + \alpha Y_L.$$

The total change in output is composed of two parts: ΔE_o the initial change in desired expenditures plus that change in desired expenditures which was induced by the change in real income. Thus

$$\Delta Y = \Delta E_o + \alpha \Delta Y$$

or $\Delta Y (1 - \alpha) = \Delta E_o$

$$\therefore \quad \Delta Y = \frac{1}{1 - \alpha} \cdot \Delta E_o$$

which is, of course, the same as the result we had before.

So far we have concentrated mainly on the arithmetic of the multiplier and the process by which a change in desired expenditures affects real output. It might be useful at this stage to summarize the economics involved in these concepts. Starting from an equilibrium situation in which desired expenditures are equal to total output, all the goods and services actually being produced are used up for various purposes; and given the behaviour and constraints determining desired expenditures (in our simple example only real income) people *want* to use up exactly that amount. Thus it is a situation in which actual expenditures are equal to desired expenditures and both are equal to actual output. Now for some reason there is a change in desired expenditures (eg because of a change in tastes). Now desired expenditures are greater than actual expenditures and greater than actual output. People cannot acquire the amount of goods and services they want to. Given our assumptions about the behaviour of output the attempt by people to equate actual expenditures with desired expenditures will lead to an increase in output – more factors of production will be used and output (and actual expenditures) will rise. However, the rise in output means that real income rises. If real income had no effect on desired expenditures the rise in real income would not introduce any complications. However, we assumed a behavioural relationship between desired expenditures and real income. The rise in real income will induce people to increase their desired expenditures by more than the initial change. This process continues until we again reach a situation in which desired expenditures equal actual expenditures and both are equal to total output. In the above discussion we implicitly assumed that output can increase, ie that there are unemployed resources available in the economy. We also ignored the whole question of how the increase in desired expenditures is translated into an increase in real output.[1]

In our previous discussion of expenditures we saw that we have a wide choice as to how to subdivide expenditures into various categories and we gave some examples of

---

[1] We did not specify any variable which is affected by the change in desired expenditures which can provide the information and incentive leading to a change in output.

possible criteria by which these categories could be defined. For many purposes it has been found useful to subdivide total desired expenditures in a closed economy into three categories; consumption (C), investment (I), and government expenditures (G). This particular subdivision has elements of all the criteria mentioned on pp. 8 and 9. The variables determining these expenditures are different and therefore to analyse these expenditures it is useful to separate them; the economic units making decisions with respect to these expenditures are different, and the purposes for which they are made are different. Thus we have by definition

$$E = C + I + G$$

and our equilibrium condition $Y = E$ becomes

$$Y = C + I + G.$$

   If we want to discuss an open economy, ie one in which foreign trade takes place, we have to add two elements. Our condition for equilibrium is still the same, ie desired expenditures have to be equal to the total amount of goods and services available to the economy. Now, however, the goods and services available to the economy consist of the output of the economy plus all those goods and services it 'receives' from other economies. Also goods and services can now be used in another way — they can be 'given' to other economies. If M represents imports and X exports our condition for equilibrium in the goods sector becomes

$$Y + M = C + I + G + X$$

or $Y = C + I + G + (X - M).$ \hfill (2.2.13)

   However, to concentrate on the understanding of the concepts used in analyzing the goods sector we shall first subdivide total desired expenditures into only two categories, consumption and investment. We can do this either by assuming that we are dealing with an economy in which these are the only two uses for goods and services or by consolidating all expenditures into these categories. With this subdivision of total expenditures the equilibrium condition for the goods sector is

$$Y = C + I.$$ \hfill (2.2.14)

At this stage it is useful to notice that the equilibrium condition above can be restated in another way, often useful for some problems. From (2.2.14)

$Y - C = I.$ (2.2.15)

If we define saving (S) as being the difference between total real income and desired consumption, ie $S \equiv Y - C$ then (2.2.15) can be restated as

$S = I.$ (2.2.16)

(2.2.16) is no more than a different way of saying the same thing as (2.2.14). It also shows the situation for which it is true that total desired expenditures are equal to total output. By our definition of S as the difference between the total quantity of goods and services produced per period time (Y) and the quantity of goods and services people want to use up for consumption (C), it measures the quantity of goods and services produced in the economy but not wanted for consumption. Thus it measures all the goods left over for other uses. With our subdivision of total expenditures, the only other use for goods is investment. Thus the condition for equilibrium, $S = I$, is identical to the one $Y = C + I$.

2.3   Consumption

As a first approximation we shall make the simplest behavioural hypothesis about the factors that determine how much people want to consume. We assume that desired consumption is only a function of current real income, ie $C = f(Y)$. This is obviously an oversimplification and we shall examine more sophisticated behavioural assumptions in chapter 8. For the purpose of simplifying the following discussion we shall also assume that consumption is a linear function of real income with some quantity independent of income.

Thus our first behavioural assumption is

$C = a + bY$ (2.3.1)

in this equation b is the marginal propensity to consume and measures the relationship between changes in consumption and changes in income.[1] For the moment we shall assume that desired investment is not dependent on any of the variables so far discussed but has some fixed value, ie

$I = I_0.$ (2.3.2)

---

[1] The marginal propensity to consume is $\frac{dC}{dY} = b$ in equation 2.3.1. The average propensity to consume is

$$\frac{C}{Y} = \frac{a}{Y} + b.$$

Substituting (2.3.1) and (2.3.2) into the equilibrium condition (equation (2.2.14))

$$Y = a + bY + I_o \tag{2.3.3}$$

solving for Y_o, the equilibrium income, we have[1]

$$Y - bY = a + I_o$$

$$Y(1 - b) = a + I_o$$

$$\therefore \; Y_o = \frac{1}{1 - b} [a + I_o]. \tag{2.3.4}$$

If for some reason investment now changes by ΔI to I_1 we have a new equilibrium income. Using the same procedure as above we get

$$Y_1 = \frac{1}{1 - b} [a + I_1]. \tag{2.3.5}$$

The change in income (ΔY) resulting from the change in investment (ΔI) is equal to (2.3.5) minus (2.3.4) which is

$$\Delta Y = \frac{1}{1 - b} \cdot \Delta I. \tag{2.3.6}$$

The multiplier in this case is $\frac{1}{1 - b}$. This is identical to what we did in more general terms in section 2.2. (pp. 10 - 11). Now, however, we specifically assume that consumption is the only element of desired expenditures which is behaviourally related to income, and therefore b measures the relationship between changes in income and changes in those desired expenditures dependent on income.[2]

---

[1] We could get exactly the same result by using the other formulation of the equilibrium condition, ie $S = I$.
Because $\quad S \equiv Y - C$

$$= Y - a - bY$$

$$= Y(1 - b) - a$$

the equilibrium condition is $S = I_o$

$$\therefore \; Y(1 - b) - a = I_o$$

$$\therefore \; Y_o = \frac{1}{1 - b} [a + I_o].$$

[2] In terms of figure 2.2.1 above and the equations there the following 'translation' can be made:

2.4   Investment

The second major category of desired expenditures we wish to examine is investment ie current expenditures on goods and services not for the purpose of satisfying current wants but to increase the potential for satisfying future wants. To formulate some useful hypothesis about the determination of desired investment we must examine the behaviour of those groups — mainly firms — making investment decisions. The reason why a firm undertakes an investment in an income-yielding real asset,[1] a machine for example, is because it expects an income stream in the future. To acquire the asset the firm can either borrow funds in the market or use its own available funds. In either case the cost to the firm of acquiring the expected income stream from the asset can be represented by the interest rate. If the firm borrows funds then the interest rate measures what it has to pay for the funds and thus what it has to pay for the income stream it acquires with the funds. If the firm uses its own funds then the interest rate measures the alternative cost of acquiring the income stream from the asset — instead of using its funds to acquire the asset the firm could lend its funds on the market at the going interest rate. Assume the price of a machine say, is £X, and the expected net income stream (after depreciation) from the machine is £Y per annum. The decision facing the firm is whether an income stream of £Y per annum is enough to compensate it for making an outlay of £X which, if borrowed, will cost the firm r per cent of £X per annum, if not borrowed could earn the firm r per cent of £X per annum. We can see that the higher the interest rate, the higher must be the expected income stream from the investment to make it worthwhile. At lower interest rates lower-yielding investments will be undertaken.[2]

$$E = C + I = a + I + bY$$

and $E_0 = a + I$ = those expenditures independent of income; $E_y = bY$ = those expenditures dependent on income.

[1] From our whole previous discussion about the role that desired expenditures play in the determination of equilibrium in the goods sector it should be clear that by investment we mean only real investment which uses up part of the current output of goods and services. Buying a bond, for example, even though it is an income-yielding asset to the individual, is not an investment from the point of view of the economy.

[2] The comparison between the income stream yielded by an investment and the cost of acquiring the income stream becomes more complicated when the income stream varies from year to year. In this case in some years the income stream may be greater than the interest cost, in some years it may be less. This problem can easily be overcome by evaluating the present value of the income stream using the market rate of interest which, as we saw above, represents the alternative cost of acquiring the income stream. If £Y_t is the expected income at time t and £V is the present value of the income stream, then

$$£V = \frac{£Y_1}{(1+r)}1 + \frac{£Y_2}{(1+r)}2 + \frac{£Y_3}{(1+r)}3 + \ldots + \frac{£Y_t}{(1+r)}t$$

(continued page 18)

Following the above discussion our first approximation of the behaviour of desired investment is that it is a function of the interest rate, ie $I = g(r)$. For simplicity let us assume a linear relationship

$$+I = g_0 - g_1 r \qquad\qquad (2.4.1)$$

In figure 2.4.1 we measure real investment on the horizontal axis and the interest rate on the vertical axis. The curve marked I represents our demand curve for real investment, ie equation (2.4.1) above.

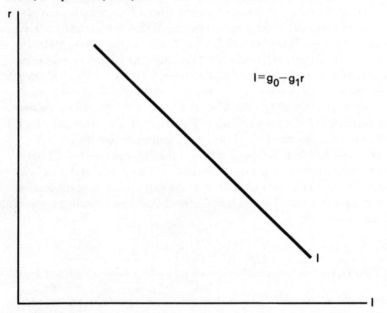

Figure 2.4.1

2.5   The equilibrium condition re-examined

We have now specified behavioural hypotheses for the two categories of expenditures into which we have subdivided total desired expenditures — consumption and investment. Substituting these behavioural hypotheses into the condition for equilibrium in the goods sector, $Y = C + I$, we have,

$$Y = a + bY + g_0 - g_1 r, \qquad\qquad (2.5.1)$$

Once £V is calculated it can be compared directly with £X, the price of acquiring the asset. If $V >$ X the investment will be undertaken, if $V < X$ it will not be undertaken.

solving for Y this becomes

$$Y = \frac{1}{1-b}[a + g_0 - g_1 r].$$ (2.5.2)

As can be seen, equation (2.5.2) is a relationship between two variables Y and r (all the other elements in the equation are behavioural constants). It shows the combinations of Y and r for which the equilibrium condition in the goods sector is satisfied, ie for which total desired expenditures, given our behavioural assumptions, will be equal to total output; or for which $S = I$. We can show both our behavioural relationships and the equilibrium condition in the following diagram.

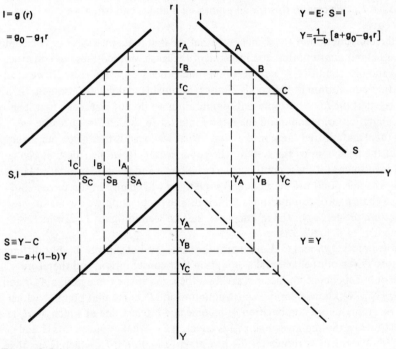

Figure 2.5.1

In the four quadrant diagram (figure 2.5.1) we measure real income per unit time on the right horizontal and bottom vertical axes. Along the top vertical axis we measure the rate of interest. Along the left horizontal axis we measure both saving and investment per unit time (this can be done because saving and investment are measured in the same units). The top left-hand quadrant represents our behavioural assumption about investment, ie the function $I = g_0 - g_1 r$. The bottom left-hand quadrant represents our behavioural assumption about consumption, ie $C = a + bY$, combined with our definition of saving, ie $S \equiv Y - C$, thus it graphs the relationship between saving and income, ie $S = -a + (1 - b) Y$. The bottom right-hand quadrant has a 45° line which represents the identity $Y \equiv Y$ (it allows the transcription of quantities from the vertical axis to the horizontal axis). In the top right-hand quadrant is the derived curve representing the equilibrium condition in the goods sector (equation (2.5.2) above) – the combinations of income and the rate of interest for which $Y = C + I$ or for which $S = I$. It is derived as follows. At an interest rate of r_A for example, desired investment is equal to I_A given the investment function shown. Our saving function shows that saving will be equal to that investment at an income level of Y_A. Transcribing that income level to the horizontal axis via the 45° line we get a point like A, ie (r_A, Y_A) at which $S_A = I_A$. We can do this for all points, eg B and C and when we join these we get the *IS* curve.

From the construction of the *IS* curve we can see that it summarizes our behavioural assumptions about consumption and investment (because we used these to construct the curve) and our condition of equilibrium in the goods sector. However, if we assume, as we do, that equilibrium in the goods sector is attainable and will be attained, then when we say that the *IS* curve represents equilibrium we do not just mean that it shows all the combinations of income and the rate of interest for which $S = I$ because we measured them and plotted them in that way. What we mean is that given our assumptions about the behaviour of the system (the goods sector) it *will* be true that saving will equal investment (at these combinations of income and the rate of interest) because if $S \neq I$ (ie at some point off the *IS* curve) something will change in the system and continue to change until equilibrium is achieved. The proposition we are making about the equilibrium properties of the *IS* curve can best be seen in figure 2.5.2 which is just the top half of figure 2.5.1.

The three points A, B and C all represent the same level of income Y_0 but different interest rates. Given our behavioural assumption that consumption, and therefore saving, are only dependent on income, saving is the same at the three points A, B and C, let us say S_0. We know from the construction of the *IS* curve that point B, which is on the curve, represents a combination of income and interest rate at which $S = I$, ie at the interest rate r_B desired investment I_B is equal to S_0. What about points A and C? At A desired investment as shown by the investment function is I_A which is less than I_B. However, as A represents the same income as B (and C) saving is the same as at B, ie S_0. Therefore at A, $S_0 > I_A$, which means that the total output of the economy is greater than desired expenditures. On the assumptions we have made about what happens to output and therefore real income in a disequilibrium situation we know that output (Y) will fall (the direction of the arrow) until equilibrium is reached. Similarly at C desired investment is equal to I_C but saving is equal to S_0 therefore $I_C > S_0$ which implies that desired expenditures are greater than total output. Again,

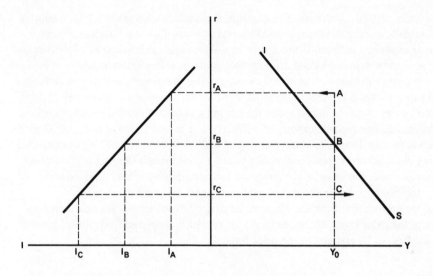

Figure 2.5.2

given our assumptions, the only thing that will happen is that output (Y) will rise till we again attain an equilibrium point, represented by some point on the *IS* curve.

To summarize. When we say that the *IS* curve shows the combinations of income and the rate of interest at which the goods sector will be in equilibrium this is not because we used some simple geometry and constructed the curve so that all points on it are points at which saving equals investment. The goods sector will be in equilibrium at these combinations of income and the interest rate because we have assumed some specific economic relationships and an equilibrium process (even though not a very satisfactory one at the moment) which lead to this conclusion.

2.6 The goods sector and the price level

Although the price level is not relevant for our condition of equilibrium in the goods sector, which is specified in terms of the quantity of goods and services, it may be relevant to our specification of the behavioural relationships determining desired expenditures.[1] Whether a change in the price level, ie all prices, will or will not affect desired expenditures depends on the behavioural relationships determining the various elements of desired expenditures. With respect to consumption, we assumed that it was

---

[1]Until we study the output and employment sector we will stick to the assumption that only desired expenditures affect output and therefore changes in the price level will only affect output if they affect desired expenditures.

behaviourally related to income. The question is therefore whether this relationship is in real terms or in money terms, ie whether real consumption is a function of real income or of money income. If the former is the case then a doubling of *all* prices (and therefore of money income also), for example, will not affect real consumption because real income stays the same. It is reasonable to assume that people's decisions about the quantity of goods and services to consume depends on real income, and we shall do so. The same question can be asked about the second element of desired expenditures — investment. Are the decisions about investment made in real terms or not, ie if all prices double will people desire the same quantity of real investment or not? We shall assume that they do. Again this seems reasonable because even though the cost of the investment has doubled, the value of the expected income stream has also doubled and it is the relationship between the two that determines real investment.

Thus we assume that both the elements of desired expenditures are unaffected by changes in the price level. Therefore the *IS* curve which is derived from these elements is also unaffected by changes in the price level.

references

ACKLEY G *Macroeconomic Theory* Collier Macmillan, Student Edition Chapters 2 and 3

BROOMAN F S *Macroeconomics* George Allen and Unwin 1971 Chapter 2

chapter 3

the money sector

In the last chapter we examined the decisions relating the flow of output and desired expenditures. In this chapter we turn to the decisions involving the allocation of wealth among different assets. This sector of decision-making is called the money sector because we concentrate on the problem of what determines the allocation of wealth between money and all other assets, which for the purpose of illustration we shall represent by bonds. We make this particular subdivision of the wealth sector because money is a very peculiar asset. As long as all individuals believe that it represents command over resources, each individual can exchange it for goods and services, even though the economy as a whole cannot acquire resources for it; money is like a myth which requires only imagination for its creation, but faith for its effectiveness. As with all other effective myths this one too arouses curiosity. Why do people hold money? What determines how much money there is to hold? What is the relationship between the quantity of money and other economic variables? Can money be used as a policy variable to affect, say, income and employment? To answer these questions we start with an intuitive discussion of equilibrium in the wealth sector (section 3.1) and go on to examine the determinants of the demand for money (section 3.2), and the supply of money (section 3.3). We then examine equilibrium in the money sector (section 3.4) and how this sector is affected by the price level (section 3.5). In the appendix (section 3.6) we examine how a liquid assets reserve ratio operates.

3.1 The wealth sector

At any point of time there exists in the economy a stock, ie some given quantity of various kinds of assets, which differ in many respects. Some assets yield an income stream whose real value is not affected by changes in the price level, for example houses, machines, and so on. The income stream of some assets consists of so many units of money per period — therefore changes in the price level change the real value of the income stream and thus the asset, for example bonds, Treasury bills, and money. The assets differ in maturities, in risk and probably in many other ways. At every point of time all these assets are held by individuals in the economy. It is useful to define equilibrium for a particular asset market as being the price or yield at which the quantity demanded of the asset is exactly equal to the quantity supplied of the asset, and equilibrium in the wealth sector as being the conglomeration of prices or yields at which there exists equilibrium in every asset market.[1] For example, in an economy in which wealth can be held in only three forms, money, bonds and houses, we would define equilibrium in the money market as being the situation in which the quantity of money demanded is equal to the quantity of money supplied in the economy, and we would define equilibrium in the bond market and the housing market analogously. Equilibrium in the wealth sector would be the situation in which all the three markets were in equilibrium.[2] To say more about the economic forces involved in all this, and what variables affect the equilibrium, we have to examine what it is that determines how much of each asset people want to hold, what determines how much of each asset is available to hold, and what forces are generated when equilibrium does not exist.

Intuitively, we can go a little further in understanding what equilibrium in the wealth sector means and whether our definition of the condition for equilibrium above is a useful one. People hold assets because assets yield a return — a flow of income of one form or another. Some assets might yield a certain number of pounds per year; some assets a service income of one form or another. For example, a house yields housing services if one lives in it, or an income of so many pounds per year if one lets it. Some assets yield a service income more difficult to describe but just as important. A painting or a diamond yields income in the form of the satisfaction (aesthetic or snob) of looking at the one and showing off the other (or vice versa). Assets also differ in the risks attached to the flow of the particular form of income generated by them, both in type and degree of risk involved. For example, holding a bond might involve the risk of a capital loss if the rate of interest changes; every asset whose yield is denominated in money terms involves a risk of changes in its value due to changes in the price level.

An individual faced by all these different assets in which he can hold his wealth will presumably allocate it among the assets in such a way as to maximize the 'income'

[1]When speaking about assets we shall sometimes talk about their prices, sometimes about their yield. For a given market rate of interest these two are uniquely related — the price of the asset is the present value of its yield discounted at the market rate of interest.

[2]By Walras law, if there are n markets connected by a budget or wealth constraint and $n - 1$ of them are in equilibrium the n'th one is also in equilibrium, it is enough, in our example, to know that two of the markets are in equilibrium to be able to say that the whole sector is in equilibrium. All this means is that if, for example, people are willing to hold the quantity of money they are holding (equilibrium in the money market) and the quantity of bonds they are holding (equilibrium in the bond market) then they must be willing to hold the quantity of houses they are holding, because if houses, bonds and money are the only ways in which one can hold wealth, then wanting to hold more of one's wealth in the form of houses means wanting to hold less in the form of bonds or money. This implies that if we know that the bond and money markets are in equilibrium, ie people are holding the amount of bonds they want to hold and the amount of money they want to hold, they must be holding the amount of houses they want to hold, ie the housing market is also in equilibrium.

yielded by his wealth, both monetary and otherwise (by income we mean here the total flow of services, in whatever form, generated by the assets). This will occur when the individual's portfolio of assets, his wealth, is allocated in such a way that he cannot increase his income (yield) by switching his wealth from one form into another or, in other words, when, on the margin the yield from each asset, in whatever form it accrues, is identical after taking account of differences in risk. Thus asset A may yield 5 per cent, asset B may yield 6 per cent yet this may be an equilibrium situation if asset B has a higher risk and the extra 1 per cent just compensates for the risk differential.[1] Applying the above discussion to a wealth sector consisting of only two assets – money and bonds – the equilibrium condition can be defined as that set of rates of returns (yields) which will make the quantity demanded of each exactly equal to the quantity supplied, and this will occur when the quantity of money demanded is equal to the quantity of money supplied (see note 2, p. 25). To examine the money sector further we have to see what determines the demand for money and what determines the supply of money. But first we must consider what to regard as 'money'.

When one tries to define exactly which set of assets is to be regarded as 'money', one can easily get involved in a scholastic debate as interesting and useful as the one on how many angels can dance on a pin. A lawyer might define money as being whatever is legal tender (in most countries currency only) and for the purpose of suing and being sued that might be a perfectly valid and useful definition. For an economist, however, it might be a completely useless definition because the economic function of money, and the reasons why people wish to hold it, might not be a function of its legal tender aspect. A checking deposit, even though not legal tender in most countries, might be considered a perfect or near-perfect substitute for currency and so should be included as money in the economist's definition of the term. To define money as any asset that can be used for the purpose of making transactions – as a medium of exchange – is also not very edifying when it comes down to measuring its quantity. In some places and for some transactions checking deposits can be used as a medium of exchange; deposit accounts can easily be converted into cash or checking deposits and used to make transactions; cars are often acceptable as a medium of exchange (when buying cars), and a £20 note is not very acceptable as a medium of exchange (when buying a bus ride). More than this, however, what is important in deciding whether we want to include a particular asset in our definition of money must depend on whether people consider that particular asset as serving the same function (ie being a good substitute for) that money serves, whatever this is. Money is usually defined as an asset which serves the function of a medium of exchange, a store of value, and a measure of value. However, the difficulty is to specify which of all the assets existing in an economy meet

---

[1] We could also say the risk avoidance of asset A (relative to asset B) is part of the service income yielded by asset A, thus the total income yielded by asset A is also 6 per cent.

these specifications, or more important, which of the assets are considered by the holders as meeting these specifications.[1] All assets do so to some extent and at some cost. The attempt to specify once and for all on some *a priori* basis exactly what money is, is bound to fail, because it is not its technical properties which are relevant but its economic properties.

A much more useful approach is to look at the problem from a different point of view. The reason why we are interested in money is because we think that its quantity has an important effect on certain economic variables, for example the price level, the level of income, and the rate of interest. Therefore, what we want to define as money is that subset of assets which does influence these variables. Of course, the larger the set of assets which must be included as 'money', the less useful will the concept be, because ultimately we shall want to know what determines the supply of money, and the larger the group of assets which are included in 'money', the more difficult this will be.[2] The specification of the functions of money and the various *a priori* definitions of money might give us some idea as to which assets to try, but the ultimate decision must be an empirical one. For the purpose of the rest of this chapter (and book), therefore, we shall define money as being currency and current account deposits. This particular definition is adopted because it has been found useful in many empirical studies relating money to those economic variables in which we are interested.

3.2   The demand for money

We shall now attempt to formulate a theory to explain why people want to hold money. The decision to hold part of one's wealth in the form of money is not costless; money, in contrast to other assets, does not yield an explicit rate of return. If on the average an individual holds £100 during a year in the form of money and the rate of interest is 5 per cent then the alternative cost to him of holding his wealth in this form rather than in the form of a bond, for example, is £5 a year. It is therefore a relevant question to ask what services money yields which leads individuals to pay a price to hold it, and what are the relevant variables entering into this decision problem.

Three general motives are usually proposed for the holding of money: the transactions motive, the speculative motive, and the precautionary motive. The first motive arises from the function of money as a medium of exchange. Most economic activity involves the exchange of goods, services, or factors, and barter is a very costly way of making exchanges. Money is an asset, which, because of its general acceptability as a

---

[1] Someone once defined money as 'money is what money does'. This defines money perfectly. The only problem is that if one wants to measure the quantity of money, the definition does not help very much.

[2] Of course it may be true that we cannot find any subset of assets which is both 'small' and has an important effect on income, the price level, and so on. In that case we would drop the distinction between 'money' and other assets.

medium of exchange, can be exchanged easily for goods and other assets. One of the reasons why people are willing to hold part of their wealth in the form of money is that it allows them to make transactions without first undergoing the costs and inconveniences of converting some other asset into money. With respect to this particular motive it seems intuitively reasonable that the two variables which would be important in determining how much money people want to hold are the volume of transactions they make, and the cost involved in holding wealth in the form of money. The first of these variables can be represented by real income because the higher real income is the greater will be the volume of transactions made. The cost of holding wealth in the form of money can be represented by the rate of interest, which shows what could be earned if wealth were held in the form of interest-bearing assets, rather than in the form of money.

The speculative motive is of a somewhat different nature. In our simple economy in which we have assumed the existence of only two assets the only way to hold wealth besides money is in the form of bonds. Bonds are promises to pay a fixed amount per period. The price of a bond depends on this fixed amount and the market rate of interest. If a bond promises to pay £50 per year and the market rate of interest is 5 per cent the price of the bond will be £1,000. If the rate of interest falls to 4 per cent, the price of the bond will rise to £1,250; if the rate of interest rises to 8 per cent the price of the bond will fall to £625.[1] A person holding his wealth in the form of bonds is thus subjected to the risk of capital losses if the rate of interest rises and capital gains if the rate of interest falls, a risk which is not present if wealth is held in the form of money.[2] The avoidance of this risk is not, however, a free good. One can avoid this risk completely by holding all of one's wealth in the form of money; changes in the rate of interest will then have no effect on its value. The price paid for avoiding the risk is that the yield on one's wealth will be zero. The choice facing the individual of whether to hold money or bonds can thus be represented as a choice between yield and risk. The higher is the proportion of wealth held in the form of bonds, the higher is the yield received by the individual from his wealth, but also the higher is the risk to which his wealth is exposed. The higher is the proportion of wealth held in the form of money, the lower is the yield received from it, but also the lower is the degree of risk to which it is exposed. The speculative motive for holding money is the motive to hold

[1] We are here assuming that the bond is a perpetuity whose price is y/r where y is the coupon yield (in our example £50 per year) and r is the market rate of interest.

[2] One must distinguish here between the risk associated with interest rate changes and expectations about interest rate changes. If an individual expects the rate of interest to change, then the expected yield from holding a bond, and therefore the cost of holding money, is the interest yield plus or minus the expected capital gain or loss. There is still, however, a risk associated with the expected yield, namely that the actual change in the interest rate will be different from the expected change, and therefore the actual capital gain or loss will be different from the expected capital gain or loss.

money rather than bonds to reduce the risk associated with the holding of wealth.

From the point of view of the speculative motive we can look at the rate of interest as the price of insuring against the risk of capital losses by switching one's wealth from bonds into money. Given an individual's tastes for risk, we would expect that the higher is the price of insuring against risk the less insurance would be bought. This means that the higher is the rate of interest the larger would be the fraction of the individual's wealth held in the form of bonds; the lower is the rate of interest the larger would be the fraction of wealth held in the form of money. Thus the demand for money associated with the speculative motive will be negatively related to the rate of interest. The discussion so far has been in terms of the allocation of a given quantity of wealth among money and bonds. The actual amount of money people will want to hold will also depend on the total quantity of wealth that is to be allocated among the two assets. For any rate of interest which determines the *fraction* of wealth to be held in the form of money, the larger the total quantity of wealth the larger will be the quantity of money demanded. We can thus represent the demand for money arising from the speculative motive as a function of the rate of interest (and the level of wealth).

The precautionary motive is much vaguer, although possibly just as important a motive for holding money as the others. When discussing the speculative motive we considered the holding of money as a means of avoiding the specific risk of changes in the interest rate. Economic activity involves many other uncertainties besides that of changes in the interest rate. Because of its general acceptability as a medium of exchange for all or most transactions, money is also a useful reserve in which to hold wealth to meet these other uncertainties. By holding money one can avoid the time and costs involved in converting other assets into money. Again we can ask what variables might be important in determining how much money people will want to hold for this purpose. As a first approximation we will use the rate of interest and the level of income. We include the rate of interest because it represents the price paid to acquire the precautionary services yielded by money. We include income because we assume that precautionary services are not an inferior good and therefore the higher is the level of income the more of this good people will want to acquire, just as with other non-inferior goods.

It may be useful to point out at this stage that in all the functions of money discussed above, money is not unique. As in all of economics the question is very seldom one of all or nothing, but one of more or less. To some extent and at some cost all assets can serve all the functions we have been discussing. If money serves these functions better than do other assets, then people will be willing to pay some price to hold money rather than other assets.

It should be emphasized that the motives for holding money discussed above might be useful to understand why people hold money at all, and what variables may be important in determining how much money they want to hold. It is, however, not particularly useful to separate out part of money as 'transactions money', part as 'speculative money', and part as 'precautionary money'. Every unit of money serves all these (and possibly other) functions simultaneously. Hence we shall not separate out different monies, but analyze the total quantity of money in the light of the previous discussion.

The above motives for holding money can be conceptually useful both for the demand for money by households (money as a consumer good — yielding services analogous to consumption services) and the demand for money by firms (money as a factor of production — yielding services analogous to those yielded by other factors of production). Firms may hold money because as a medium of exchange it allows them to make transactions (the transactions motive); holding other assets involves a risk of capital losses (the speculative motive); and holding money may, for example, allow them to hold smaller inventories of goods and still meet any unexpected changes in demand (the precautionary motive). Again it seems reasonable to use the rate of interest and the level of income as a first approximation to the variables determining how much money firms will want to hold. The former is used because it represents the alternative cost of holding money rather than other assets, the latter is used because the general level of output is important in determining the demand for all factors of production, including money.

Following the above discussion about the motives for holding money we shall make the behavioural assumption that the demand for money is positively related to the level of real income and negatively related to the rate of interest, or more formally $m^d = f(r, Y)$.[1] We represent this behavioural assumption in figure 3.2.1.

On the horizontal axis we measure the quantity of money demanded and on the vertical axis the rate of interest. Three demand curves are shown for income levels Y_1, Y_2, and Y_3 where $Y_3 > Y_2 > Y_1$. The ordering of these curves follows from our behavioural assumption about the relationship between the quantity of money demanded and the level of income.

3.3   The supply of money
Given that we have defined money as being currency and current account deposits in commercial banks, there are at least two groups of economic units whose behaviour we have to examine when studying the determinants of the supply of money — the suppliers of currency and the suppliers of deposits. In most countries the only supplier of currency (if we ignore forgery) is some central authority, for example the issue department of the Bank of England in the United Kingdom. We can therefore treat the

[1] Following our discussion of the speculative motive we should include wealth in this function. For the moment we assume that wealth is given because we want to concentrate on the links introduced into our model via real income and the interest rate. For a further discussion of this problem see the appendix of chapter 6.

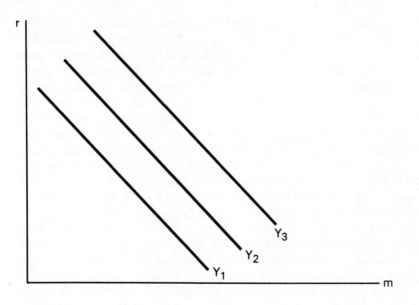

Figure 3.2.1

supply of currency as being exogenous to the system, possibly affecting the economic system but not being affected by it, except insofar as the monetary authority decides it wants to be affected.[1] The supply of bank deposits is not so simple. To see how this is determined we have to examine the behaviour of the suppliers – the banks – and the constraints within which they must operate.

In most countries the banking system operates on a partial reserve basis – banks have a legal requirement to hold some fraction of their deposits in the form of some particular assets, which we shall call reserve assets. This means that the *maximum* quantity of deposits that the banks can 'create' depends on two factors, the total quantity of the reserve assets available to the economy and the amount of the reserve assets available to the banking sector of the economy. The first of these is determined by the suppliers of the reserve assets, the second by the various economic units within the economy wishing to hold the assets and the variables that are relevant to this decision. The allocation of the reserve assets between the banking sector and the non-banking sector is important because only the reserve assets held by the banking sector can be used as reserves for the creation of deposits by the banks.

To understand exactly what is meant by the process of deposit creation, and the relationship between this process and the quantity of the reserve assets available to the

[1]This is not strictly true in a modern financial system. We discuss this problem in more detail below.

banking sector, we shall first examine the simplest case of an economy in which the
only reserve asset is currency, whose supply is controlled by a central authority. We
shall assume that banks must hold at least 10 per cent of their deposits in the form of
currency (what they do with the rest is up to them). We shall also assume that the
public (the non-banking sector of the economy) is willing to hold all of its money in
the form of deposits, and does not wish to hold currency at all, once it has the oppor-
tunity to have bank accounts. Let us start with a situation in which no banking system
exists as yet, and the amount of currency (C_u) in the economy is £100. We now introduce a banking system with the specifications mentioned above. For the purpose of
illustration let us assume that there are two banks, *A* and *B*. The process of deposit
creation is best illustrated by looking at the balance sheets of the three parties involved
in our example – bank *A*, bank *B*, and the public. Table 3.3.1 (page 34) shows the
balance sheets of these groups. The assets columns for the banks are divided into two
subcolumns marked C_B and *L*. The first represents the currency held by the banks, the
second the loans the banks make if they so wish. The liability columns of the banks
contain deposits only, because these are the only liabilities of the banks in our simplified model. In the balance sheet of the public, assets are represented by currency (C_P)
and deposits (D), liabilities by the loans from the banks. The first column on the left
represents the various steps in the process of deposits creation. A plus in front of a
number in the body of the table shows an increase in that particular item, a minus
represents a decrease. For each step read across for what happens.

Step (a) shows the situation of the economy before the creation of banks. The public
has £100 of currency and that is all. Step (b) represents the opening of our banking
system. The public deposits its £100 of currency in bank *A* and so it is credited with
£100 of deposits. At this point all that has happened is that the public has exchanged
£100 of currency for £100 of deposits, and the bank has exchanged £100 of deposits
(a liability to it) for £100 of currency.[1] The money supply of the non-banking sector
of the economy is still £100 but now it is all in the form of deposits (this follows our
assumption above that the public wants to hold all of its money in the form of deposits).
At this stage, however, the bank has only £100 of liabilities (deposits) and is holding
£100 of assets (currency). These assets are not earning any return for the bank so we
shall assume that the bank will invest them in some form of income-yielding asset. Let
us assume that the bank uses the currency to make a loan to some member of the
public. On our assumption the legal reserve requirement is 10 per cent so the bank
cannot lend the full £100; the maximum it can lend is £90, retaining £10 as reserves
against the £100 of deposits. Of course the bank can, if it so wishes, keep more than

---

[1] All that has happened is that one myth has been exchanged for another. Instead of exchanging
goods and services for a green piece of paper (a bank note), people now exchange goods and services
for a pink piece of paper (a cheque).

£10 in the form of currency; however, we shall assume that it lends the full amount it is allowed to lend. This is shown in step (c) of the table. On the bank's balance sheet currency goes down by £90, loans go up by £90; on the balance sheet of the public currency goes up by £90 (someone received the loan) and liabilities to the banking sector also go up by £90. At this stage the bank is in equilibrium. It is holding the amount of reserves required by law, and cannot lend out any more even if it wanted to: it could of course reduce its loans outstanding, but we assumed that it wanted to lend the full £90. The total money supply is now £190; the public has £100 of deposits and £90 of currency. On our assumption about the public's desired currency holding, however, this is not an equilibrium situation for them. They will take the £90 of currency and exchange it for deposits by depositing it in bank B (let us say). This is shown in step (d) in the table. This step is identical to step (b) except that £90 is involved in the exchange instead of £100 (and bank B instead of bank A). Now, however, bank B is not in equilibrium. It has £90 of currency which is earning nothing, but needs only £9 of currency as a reserve against the £90 of deposits. Let us therefore assume that it lends the difference of £81. This is shown in step (e) of the table which is identical to step (c) (except for the amounts and the banks involved). At this point the money supply is equal to £271; £190 of deposits and £81 of currency. Now, however, the public is not in equilibrium on our assumption about its desired currency holding. The process described above will thus continue until everyone, the banks and the public, is in equilibrium.

The banks will be in equilibrium when they do not have any excess reserves – they do not hold more currency than they want to, or less currency than they need to, given the reserve requirement. The public will be in equilibrium when they are holding the amount of currency they want to, in our example none. Given our assumptions about the behaviour of the banks and the public the equilibrium conditions described above imply that the whole of the currency is held by the banks, and that this amount is equal to the required reserves against the outstanding deposits. With a 10 per cent reserve requirement this means that the amount of deposits outstanding is equal to £1,000. Thus, the introduction of the banking system has converted a money supply of £100, consisting only of currency, into a money supply of £1,000, consisting only of deposits. This outcome is shown at the bottom of the table in the row marked *total*. Total currency in the two banks is equal to £100; total loans of the banks are equal to £900, and total deposits to £1,000.[1]

Two points should be noticed at this stage. First, even though in our example the

---

[1] The arithmetic to arrive at these results is quite simple. The total quantity of deposits equals (see deposits column of public's assets in table 3.3.1)
$$C_u + C_u(1-\rho) + C_u(1-\rho)^2 + C_u(1-\rho)^3 \ldots.$$
where ρ is the fraction of deposits held as reserves by the banks (in our case 10 per cent). This equals
$$C_u[1 + (1-\rho) + (1-\rho)^2 + (1-\rho)^3 \ldots.]$$

(continued page 34)

Table 3.3.1

	PUBLIC			BANK A			BANK B		
	Assets		Liabilities	Assets		Liabilities	Assets		Liabilities
	C_P	D	L	C_B	L	D	C_B	L	D
(a)	100								
(b)	- 100	+ 100		+ 100		+ 100			
(c)	+ 90		+ 90	- 90	+ 90				
(d)	- 90	+ 90					+ 90		+ 90
(e)	+ 81		+ 81				- 81	+ 81	
(f)	- 81	+ 81		+ 81		+ 81			
Total	0	1,000	900	100			1,000		

banks used their currency to make loans to the public, this is not at all necessary for the process of deposit creation. Exactly the same result would occur if instead of using the currency to make loans the banks used it to buy bonds or any other asset from the public. The only difference would be that in the bank's balance sheet the asset increasing would be an item called bonds rather than loans (both of which are accounts receivable), and in the public's balance sheet we would have an item called bonds on the assets side which would decrease at each stage by the same amount by which, in our example, the loans item (a liability) increases. Thus the public would be exchanging one asset for another (deposits for bonds) instead of exchanging an asset for a liability (deposits for loans). The other point to be noticed is that even though banks are the suppliers of deposits, the amount they can supply depends on the quantity of currency

The expression in the square brackets is a geometric progression whose sum (because $(1 - \rho) < 1$) is $\frac{1}{1 -(1 - \rho)}$. Thus the whole expression is equal to $C_u \cdot \frac{1}{\rho} = £1,000$ in our example.

(the reserve asset) in the system. Thus suppliers of currency not only determine the supply of currency, but can also control the supply of deposits.

Two complications are added when we move from the particular example presented above to a more general framework for the analysis of the determinants of the money supply. First, the set of assets which can be used as reserves against deposits consists of more than currency in some cases and does not contain currency in others. Second, the allocation of the reserve assets among the banking and the non-banking sectors is more complicated than that presented in our example and, not surprisingly, the complication increases as the number of assets which can serve as reserves increases. In both the United Kingdom and the United States the central bank (the Bank of England in the UK, the Federal Reserve in the US) acts as a bankers' bank, where individual banks hold deposits which are used, among other things, for inter-bank clearing arrangements.[1] These deposits count as a reserve asset. In the United States the currency held by banks (called vault cash) also counts as a reserve against deposits, but in the United Kingdom it does not. However, currency and bankers' deposits at the central bank are substitutable on demand, just as private deposits (the public's deposits at the banks) and currency are substitutable on demand. If a bank wants currency, either because it wants to hold more vault cash or because the public wants to hold more currency and so is exchanging its deposits for currency, the bank can cash its deposits at the central bank for currency.[2]

In the United States the reserve requirement is stated in terms of the deposits held by banks at the central bank and the vault cash of the banks, ie banks must hold some fraction of their liabilities in the form of deposits at the central bank or vault cash. In the United Kingdom things are more complicated. Essentially there are two types of reserve requirement. First, some fraction of the banks' liabilities must be held in the form of deposits at the central bank. This is called the cash ratio.[3] Second, some fraction of their liabilities must be held in the form of 'liquid' assets which consist of bankers' deposits at the central bank, Treasury bills, call money and some short-term bills. In the appendix we examine the working of the 'liquid assets' reserve requirement; here we shall look at the cash ratio — how it works and how it affects the supply of money.

Given that bankers' deposits at the central bank (D_B) and currency (C_u) are sub-

---

[1] These are arrangements by which the actual process of transferring accounts among individuals is carried out. When a person with a deposit account in bank A, say, writes a cheque to a person with a deposit account in bank B, the actual transfer is made by debiting the account of bank A in the central bank and crediting that of bank B.

[2] In economies with advanced financial systems this is the way in which currency actually comes into circulation.

[3] Until September 1971 the cash ratio in the UK was 8 per cent. Since that date there is no specific cash ratio but banks have agreed to have a cash ratio of 1½ per cent.

stitutable on demand, the total quantity of reserve assets potentially available in the economy equals $D_B + C_u$. This is true whether currency held by banks does or does not count as a reserve against deposits, because banks can always exchange currency for bankers' deposits which do count as a reserve. However, what is relevant for deposit creation is not the total quantity of the reserve asset in the economy but the quantity available to the banks. We have to subtract from the total quantity that part which does not act as reserves against deposits, either because it is not held by the banks or because even if held by the banks it is legally not countable as a reserve. Let C_p be the amount of currency which is not used as reserves against deposits. What is included in C_p depends on the particular legal arrangement. In the United States C_p is the currency held by the private non-banking sector of the economy, because the currency held by the banking sector does count as part of their reserves. In the United Kingdom C_p is the currency held by both the non-banking sector *and* the banking sector because vault cash does not count as a reserve against deposits. In both cases the total amount of the reserve asset available as reserves to the banking sector is $D_B + C_u - C_p$.

Let us assume that the amount of currency the 'public' wants to hold (C_p) is some fraction of their deposits, say $C_p = cD$, and the banks want to hold a fraction (ρ) of their liabilities (the deposits of the public) in the form of the reserve asset. The fraction must, of course, be at least equal to the legal reserve requirement. As before, we define money as being the currency held by the 'public' plus the deposits in the banks.[1]
We thus have

$$M = C_p + D$$

but $C_p = cD$

$$\therefore M = D\,(c + 1). \tag{3.3.1}$$

From our earlier discussion we know that the quantity of deposits created by banks is equal to the quantity of the reserve asset they hold divided by the reserve ratio (see note 1, p. 33). Thus

$$D = [D_B + C_u - C_p]\,\frac{1}{\rho}$$

$$= [D_B + C_u - cD]\,\frac{1}{\rho}$$

---

[1] What we include as the 'public', and therefore what we include in C_p depends on the particular legal arrangement. See the discussion in the previous paragraph.

$$\therefore D\,(\rho + c) = C_u + D_B$$

$$\therefore D = \frac{1}{(c + \rho)}\ [D_B + C_u]\,. \tag{3.3.2}$$

Substituting equation (3.3.2) into equation (3.3.1) we have (remembering that $C_p = cD$)

$$M = \frac{c + 1}{c + \rho}\ [D_B + C_u]$$

or $M = h\ [D_B + C_u]$ where $h = \dfrac{c + 1}{c + \rho}$.

We can see that this formula gives the same result as we got in our simple example above if we assume, as we did there, that $c = 0$ and $D_B = 0$. We can also see that even in this general case the quantity of money in the system depends on the quantity of the reserve assets (in this case $C_u + D_B$). By controlling the quantity of the reserve assets one can control the quantity of money. However, the total $C_u + D_B$ can only be changed by some transaction between the monetary authority and the private sector; no transaction purely within the private sector will affect this total. It is clear that no transaction within the private non-banking sector can change the quantity of currency in the economy. A single individual can reduce his currency holdings by buying goods or assets from other individuals but this just transfers currency from one individual to another, leaving the total unchanged. A single bank can reduce its deposits at the central bank by buying a bond or making a loan, but this only transfers the deposit to another bank leaving the total of bankers' deposits at the central bank unchanged.[1] If all individuals want to hold more currency they can do so, because we assumed that currency and bankers' deposits were substitutable on demand, but this will still not affect the total $C_u + D_B$; the rise in C_u is exactly offset by the fall in D_B. Thus this particular transaction between the central bank and the private sector has no effect on the total quantity of the reserve assets. The situation is different, however, if the central bank buys or sells bonds to the private sector (whether banking or non-banking

[1] This inability of the banking sector to change the quantity of the reserve asset should not be confused with the ability of the banks to change the fraction of deposits they hold in the form of reserves. If all banks attempt to hold a greater fraction of deposits in the form of reserves, the attempts by each bank to increase its reserves (by selling bonds or cancelling loans) will lead not to a change in the quantity of reserves but to a change in the quantity of deposits in the system, thus changing the ratio of reserves to deposits. This can be seen by working out what would happen in table 3.3.1 above if all banks decided to hold 20 per cent reserves against deposits rather than the 10 per cent we assumed there.

is immaterial). A sale of bonds by the central bank reduces the total quantity of the reserve assets, a purchase of bonds increases it; both of these operations (known as open market operations) change D_B without any effect on C_u.[1] Given that only open market operations affect the total quantity of the reserve assets ($C_u + D_B$), the central bank which can control these transactions can also control the quantity of the reserve asset, and via this the quantity of money in the economy.

So far we have looked at the arithmetic of the money supply given the particular constraint of the necessity of holding reserves against deposits. The economic analysis comes in when examining the two behavioural variables c and ρ in our formula and seeing what determines their values; c is determined by the private non-banking sector which decides how to allocate its money between currency and deposits, ρ is determined by the private banking sector which decides on the reserve ratio between the reserve asset and deposits. Even though the minimum reserve ratio is determined by law, which for given $C_u + D_B$ means that the maximum quantity of deposits is determined by law, the actual ratio can always be greater than the minimum. Even without the law, banks would want to hold some amount of reserves to avoid the risk of illiquidity – of not being able to pay out if someone wanted to convert their deposit into cash. How much reserves they would want to hold depends on the probability of people cashing in deposits and the cost to the bank of holding assets in the form of non-income yielding assets (the reserve assets) as opposed to other assets. This cost is higher, the higher the rate of interest. Thus we would expect that the higher is the rate of interest the smaller would be the proportion of their assets banks would hold as reserves, and therefore the larger would be the amount of deposits supplied for any given $C_u + D_B$ and c. This could only continue up to the point where the banks were constrained by the minimum legal reserve requirement.

As far as c, our other behavioural variable, is concerned we shall assume that, at least in the short run, it is not affected by any of the variables in our model. Summarizing our discussion of the supply of money, we shall assume that the quantity of money supplied is positively related to the rate of interest up to some point (the point at which the banks, reserve ratio is equal to the minimum legal requirement) and then becomes perfectly inelastic. This is, of course, true for any given quantity of the reserve asset available to the economy. Any change in the quantity of the reserve asset will shift the whole supply curve.

---

[1] This occurs in the following way: when the central bank buys a bond from an individual, he receives a cheque for the amount of purchase. When he deposits the cheque in his bank and the bank presents the cheque to the central bank, the bank's account at the central bank is credited and, given that the account of no other bank is debited, D_B goes up.

3.4   Equilibrium in the money sector

We can now put together our analysis of the money sector — the demand for money and the supply of money. This is done in figure 3.4.1. On the horizontal axis we measure the quantity of money, on the vertical axis the rate of interest. The three

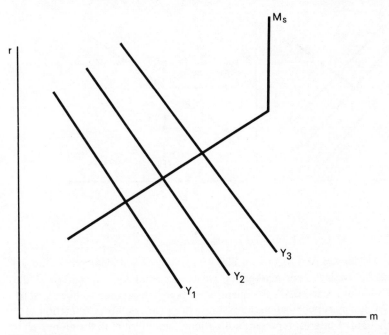

Figure 3.4.1

curves marked Y_1, Y_2, Y_3 represent three demand curves for money for various levels of income ($Y_3 > Y_2 > Y_1$), thus summarizing our behavioural assumption about the demand for money $m^d = f(r, Y)$. The curve marked M^s is the supply curve of money, for some given quantity of the reserve assets available to the economy. This curve is upward sloping up to some point because the higher the interest rate the smaller will be the proportion of their deposits banks will want to hold in the form of the reserve assets (see above), and therefore the greater will be the total quantity of deposits created by banks and thus the total quantity of money. The curve becomes perfectly inelastic at that point where the reserve ratio cannot be reduced any further because of the legal minimum reserve requirement.

We can see from figure 3.4.1 that equilibrium in the money sector, defined as the situation at which the quantity of money demanded is equal to the quantity of money supplied, can occur at various combinations of income and the rate of interest. We represent this dependence of equilibrium in the money sector on income and the rate of interest in figure 3.4.2 (b). On the horizontal axis we measure income, on the vertical axis the rate of interest. The curve marked *LM* represents all the combinations of income and the rate of interest at which the money sector is in equilibrium.

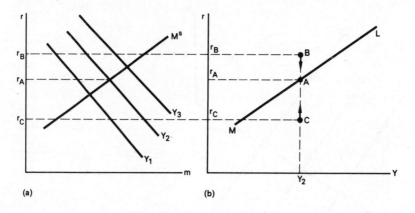

Figure 3.4.2

Figure 3.4.2(b) is derived from figure 3.4.2(a) very simply. When income is Y_2, so the relevant demand curve is the one marked Y_2, we can see from 3.4.2(a) that, when the supply curve is the one marked M^s, the quantity of money demanded will be equal to the quantity of money supplied at an interest rate of r_A; hence this combination of income and the rate of interest represent a situation of equilibrium in the money sector. We can do this for all possible combinations of income and the interest rate, and by joining these points we get the *LM* curve.

We can also use figure 3.4.2 to see why the *LM* curve represents equilibrium in the money sector, and what forces will be generated at any point off the curve. Take points *A, B,* and *C* in figure 3.4.2(b), all of which represent the same income level Y_2, and therefore the demand curve for money in figure 3.4.2(a) relevant to all these points is the one marked Y_2. Point *B* represents a situation in which income is Y_2 and the rate of interest is r_B. In figure 3.4.2(a) we can see that this combination implies an excess supply of money; people are holding a higher proportion of their wealth in the form of money than they want to. They will therefore try to get 'rid' of their money hold-ings by substituting money for other assets, in our case bonds. The attempt by every-body to do this will drive up the price of bonds and thus lower the rate of interest. This force exerted in the money sector at the disequilibrium point *B* is shown by the arrow at point *B* in figure 3.4.2(b). At the combination of income and rate of interest repre-sented by point $C(Y_2, r_C)$ we can see from figure 3.4.2(a) that there is an excess demand for money. The attempt by individuals to acquire more money by selling some of their other assets, in our case bonds, means that the price of these will fall, which implies that the rate of interest will rise. This is shown by the arrow at *C*. Only at point *A* (which is on the *LM* curve) is it true that the quantity of money demanded is equal to the quantity of money supplied and the money sector is in equilibrium.

3.5   The money sector and the price level
At this point it is useful to examine the relationship between the money sector and the general price level. Even though we have not yet put together all the various aspects of the economy, and therefore cannot yet say what determines the price level, we can still ask how the price level and changes in it affect the money sector, just as we did with the goods sector at the end of chapter 2. To answer this question we have to examine what effects the price level has on the two behavioural functions which together determine equilibrium in the money sector — the demand for money and the supply of money. As far as the demand for money is concerned the issue is whether behaviourally people's decisions with respect to how much money they want to hold are determined on the basis of real values or nominal values. We assumed that the demand for money was a function of the rate of interest and the level of real income. We are now asking what would happen if, for example, all prices doubled and money income also doubled leaving real income the same. Would the demand for nominal money also double, or would the nominal quantity of money demanded remain the same?

If we look at the discussion of the various motives for holding money (p. 27) we see that at least for two of the motives — the transactions and the precautionary motives — it seems reasonable to assume that people take into account the real quantity of money in relation to real income. If all prices double, for example, the money value of all transactions also doubles and it would require twice as much nominal money to make the same transactions — to trade the same quantity of goods. Also with respect to the precautionary motive, with all prices doubling the same quantity of nominal money will only act as a reserve for half the quantity of goods and services as before. We shall therefore assume that behaviourally people are interested in the real quantity of money when deciding how to allocate their wealth between money and other assets. Thus in our demand for money, $m^d = f(r, Y)$, m^d is the real quantity of money (the nominal quantity divided by a price index) and Y is real income.[1]

---

[1] The speculative motive is more problematic. In our discussion of this motive we assumed the existence of only money and bonds. A doubling of the price level, say, will halve the real quantity of both money and bonds without changing the proportion of money to bonds. Therefore it should not lead to a change in the demand for nominal money. However, we have simplified greatly. If the allocation of wealth among real assets and financial assets is determined in a similar way to that of the allocation of wealth among money and bonds discussed above, then a doubling of the price level, say, which reduces the real quantity of financial assets relative to real assets, may lead to a

As far as the supply of money is concerned the problem is different. We treated the supply of money, at least as a first approximation, as being determined by the authorities through their control over the quantity of the reserve asset. However, the authorities only control the nominal quantity of the reserve asset, therefore the nominal quantity of money. What this implies is that a change in all prices (and money incomes) will change the real quantity of money supplied, but will leave the real quantity of money demanded unchanged, or equivalently that it will change the nominal quantity of money demanded but leave the nominal quantity of money supplied unchanged. Our equilibrium condition for the money sector is still the same as before – the quantity of money demanded must be equal to the quantity of money supplied both in real and in nominal terms. However, if we now express the money sector in real terms we will have different supply curves for different price levels. If we measure the money sector in nominal terms we will have different demand curves for different price levels. In both cases we will have different equilibrium points for different price levels. In figure 3.5.1 we measure the real quantity of money on the horizontal axis and the rate of interest on the vertical axis, and show three demand curves for real money balances at three different levels of real income where $Y_3 > Y_2 > Y_1$. The two supply curves show the supply of real money balances at two different price levels P_1, P_2 (where $P_2 > P_1$) for some given quantity of nominal money supplied M^s.

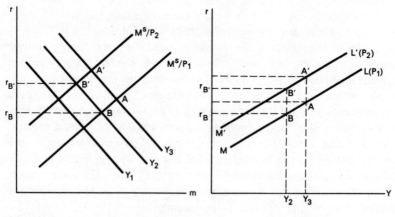

Figure 3.5.1   Figure 3.5.2

doubling of the nominal amount of all financial assets demanded including money. So even on account of this motive the demand for money would be specified in real terms. Of course, for our purpose it is not necessary that a change in the price level of a given proportion should lead to a change in the demand for nominal money of the same proportion. As long as a change in the price level leads to some change (in the same direction) in the demand for nominal money our conclusion about the dependence of equilibrium in the money sector on the price level would hold.

In figure 3.5.2 we derive the *LM* curves for the two levels of prices. As the price level moves from P_1 to P_2 the supply curve of real money moves from the one marked $\dfrac{M^s}{P_1}$ to the one marked $\dfrac{M^s}{P_2}$; the demand curves, however, are not affected by the change in the price level (see above). We therefore have a different set of equilibrium points and so a different *LM* curve for each price level.

3.6   Appendix

When we discussed the relationship between the quantity of reserve assets and control over the money supply in a partial reserve banking system, we saw that two questions were important. The first was, who determines the supply of the reserve assets? The second was, what determines the allocation of the reserve assets among the banking and the non-banking sector? The latter question was important because is is only the reserve assets held by the banking sector which can act as reserves against deposits. The same two questions are important when we examine the effects of a liquid assets reserve requirement on the control of the money supply. We shall first consider a liquid assets requirement in general and then turn to a description of the current liquid assets requirement in the UK.

Assume there are three assets A^1, A^2, A^3, which can be used by the banks as reserves against deposits. The quantity of A^1 *supplied to the economy*, call it Q^1, is controlled by a central authority and is held by the banking sector (Q_B^1) and the non-banking sector (Q_P^1). The quantities of A^2 and A^3 in the economy (Q^2 and Q^3) are determined by decisions taken by the private sector, both bank and non-bank. We shall assume that A^2 and A^3 are held only by the banking sector. Thus the quantities of A^2 and A^3 held by the banking sector depend on the demand for these assets by the banking sector and the supply of these assets by the non-banking sector. The question we want to answer is the following. What control do the authorities have over the money supply via their control over the quantity of A^1 in the economy?

Let L be the liquid assets reserve ratio, ie the banks must hold L per cent of their deposits in the form of the reserve assets A^1, A^2, A^3. By analogous procedure to that used when discussing the cash ratio (p. 36) we have

$$D = \frac{1}{L}\,[Q_B^1 + Q^2 + Q^3].$$

However $Q_B^1 = Q^1 - Q_P^1$

$$\therefore D = \frac{1}{L}\,[Q^1 - Q_P^1 + Q^2 + Q^3] \qquad\qquad (3.6.1)$$

$$\text{and } \frac{dD}{dQ^1} = \frac{1}{1}\left[1 - \frac{dQ_P^1}{dQ^1} + \frac{dQ^2}{dQ^1} + \frac{dQ^3}{dQ^1}\right] \tag{3.6.2}$$

Equation (3.6.2) says that the change in deposits resulting from a change in the total quantity of A^1 supplied to the economy depends on the effect that the change in quantity has on the non-bank holdings of A^1 (second term in brackets) and the banks' holdings of A^2 and A^3 (third and fourth terms in brackets). If all of these were zero, implying that the change in A^1 is absorbed completely by the banks, *and* that there is no offsetting effect on the banks' holdings of the other reserve assets, we would get the full multiplier effect, ie $\frac{dD}{dQ^1} = \frac{1}{1}$.

To go a little further, let us assume that A^1, A^2 and A^3 are related assets and therefore the quantities supplied and demanded of these assets, by the private sector, depend on their yields (r^1, r^2, r^3).

$$\text{Let } \frac{dQ^i}{dQ^1} = \frac{dr^i}{dQ^1} \cdot \frac{dQ^i}{dr^i}$$

$$\text{and } \eta_{i1} = \frac{dQ^i}{dr^1} \cdot \frac{r^1}{Q^i} \qquad \text{for } i = 1, 2, 3. \tag{3.6.3}$$

Substituting these expressions into (3.6.2) above we have

$$\frac{dD}{dQ^1} = \frac{1}{1}\left[1 - \frac{1}{\eta_{11}}\left[\eta_{11}^P \frac{Q_P^1}{Q^1} - \eta_{21}\frac{Q^2}{Q^1} - \eta_{31}\frac{Q^3}{Q^1}\right]\right] \tag{3.6.4}$$

$$\text{and } \frac{dD}{dQ^1} \gtrless \frac{1}{1} \text{ as } \frac{1}{\eta_{11}}\left[\eta_{11}^P \frac{Q_P^1}{Q^1} - \eta_{21}\frac{Q^2}{Q^1} - \eta_{31}\frac{Q^3}{Q^1}\right] \lessgtr 0. \tag{3.6.5}$$

The elasticities in (3.6.4) and (3.6.5) have the following meaning: η_{11} is the elasticity of demand for A^1 by both the banking and the non-banking sector. Its size determines the percentage change in the yield of A^1 (r^1) for a given percentage change in the total quantity of A^1 supplied. η_{11}^P is the elasticity of demand of the non-banking sector of the economy for A^1. It determines the percentage change in the quantity demanded of A^1 by the non-banking sector for a given percentage change in the yield of A^1. η_{21} and η_{31} are more complicated. They measure the percentage change in the quantities of A^2 and A^3 *held* by the banking sector for a given percentage change in the yield of A^1. Their size depends on both the cross elasticity of demand and of supply of A^2 and A^3 with respect to the yield on A^1.

We can see from equation (3.6.5) that whether an increase, say, in the quantity of A^1, the asset controlled by the authorities will lead to an increase or a decrease in the quantity of deposits depends on the various substitution possibilities among the reserve assets. If we knew the magnitudes of the various elasticities, and if these were relatively constant, then one could control the quantity of money by controlling the quantity of A^1. If on the other hand these elasticities were very variable and therefore difficult to predict then control of the money supply via control of A^1 would become very difficult.

Currently in the UK the liquid assets reserve ratio (1 in the above discussion) is 12½ per cent. There are six assets qualifying as reserve assets: (a) balances with the Bank of England; (b) British government and Northern Ireland government Treasury bills; (c) British government stocks with one year or less to maturity; (d) company tax reserve certificates; (e) money at call with the London money market; (f) local authority bills and commercial bills eligible for rediscount at the Bank of England. Of the six categories of assets the supply of (a), (b), (c) and (d) is controlled by the authorities, and therefore these are represented by A^1 in our previous discussion. (e) is determined by the supply of call money by the banking sector and the demand for call money by the London money market (essentially the discount houses). (f) is determined by the supply of these assets by local authorities and the relevant commercial firms and the demand for these assets by the banks.

references

BAUMOL W J 'The Transactions Demand for Cash: An Inventory Theoretic Approach' *Quarterly Journal of Economics* November 1952.

COPPOCK D and GIBSON N 'The Volume of Deposits and the Cash and Liquid Assets Ratios' *The Manchester School* September 1963.

FRIEDMAN M 'The Quantity Theory of Money - A Restatement' in M.G. Mueller (ed.) *Readings in Macroeconomics* Holt, Rinehart and Winston 1966.

LAIDLER D *The Demand for Money: Theories and Evidence* International 1969.

NEWLYN W T *Theory of Money* Clarendon Press, Oxford 1971.

SAYERS R S *Modern Banking* Clarendon Press, Oxford 1967.

TOBIN J 'Liquidity Preference as Behaviour Towards Risk' *Review of Economic Studies* Feburary 1958.

chapter 4

the goods and money sectors

In the last few chapters we separately analyzed two sectors involving two major types of economic decision-making — the decisions about the allocation of the flow of output, and those about the allocation of wealth. We know, however, that in our model these sectors are interrelated. Desired investment was assumed to be a function of the rate of interest, which is the equilibrating variable in the money sector. The demand for money was assumed to be a function of real income, which is 'determined' in the goods sector. The rate of interest is thus a linking variable transmitting changes in the money sector to the goods sector, and income a linking variable transmitting changes in the goods sector to the money sector. We shall now look at this interrelationship in more detail and examine the concept of general equilibrium in the whole economy, consisting so far of the two sectors we have examined.

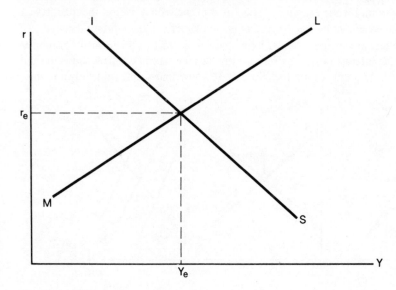

Figure 4.1

Figure 4.1 is a summary of equilibrium in the two sectors. The *IS* curve represents all the combinations of income and the rate of interest at which the goods sector is in equilibrium — at which total desired expenditures are equal to the total output of the economy. The *LM* curve shows the combinations of real income and the rate of interest at which the money sector is in equilibrium — at which the quantity of money demanded is equal to the quantity of money supplied. For the whole economy to be in equilibrium both sectors must be in equilibrium simultaneously. This will occur at only one combination of real income and the rate of interest r_e and Y_e in figure 4.1. At this combination of income and the rate of interest there is no tendency for anything to change; individuals are in equilibrium in their allocation of wealth among different assets, and in their allocation of output among different uses.

Even though in this book we are not interested in the problem of economic dynamics — the paths by which economic variables move from a disequilibrium position to one of equilibrium — it is nevertheless important to understand what economic forces are generated in disequilibrium, which combine to bring the system back to equilibrium. In figure 4.2 the centre panel represents the equilibrium conditions for the goods and money sectors. The right panel shows the money sector from which we derived the *LM* curve in the centre panel; and the left panel shows the desired investment schedule which together with the consumption function (not shown in the figure) was used to derive the *IS* schedule in the centre panel. Point *A*, showing a combination of real income and a rate of interest of Y_2 and r_e respectively, represents a situation of general equilibrium for the economy. At point *A* in the money sector, the quantity of money demanded shown by the demand curve marked Y_2 — the relevant demand curve for the real income represented by point *A* — is equal to the quantity of money supplied. At the interest rate r_e desired investment is equal to I_A; this is shown on the left-hand panel. As point *A* is on the *IS* curve we know that saving (not shown in the

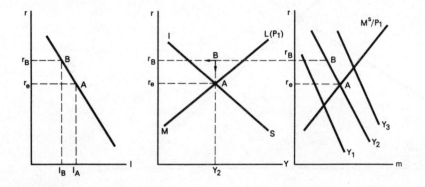

Figure 4.2

figure) generated by a real income of Y_2 is also equal to I_A, because every point on the *IS* curve represents a situation at which saving is equal to desired investment.

Let us now consider point B in the centre panel showing a combination of real income and interest rate of Y_2 and r_B respectively. We want to examine what forces would be generated in the system if the economy found itself in the situation represented by point B, and how these forces would operate to bring the economy back to equilibrium. Without looking any further we know that at point B neither the goods nor the money sectors are in equilibrium, because point B is off both the *IS* and *LM* curves. Therefore something will have to change in both sectors. Looking at the money sector in the right panel we see that at the combination of income and the rate of interest represented by point B the quantity of money supplied is greater than the quantity of money demanded. Individuals will be attempting to re-allocate their wealth from money into bonds, thus forcing the rate of interest down. The arrow pointing down at B in the centre panel represents this tendency. Looking at the left panel we see that at an interest rate of r_B desired investment is equal to I_B. However, when real income is Y_2 we know that saving is equal to I_A, because we assumed that saving is a function of real income only, therefore saving at point B is the same as at point A. Thus in the goods sector point B represents a situation in which desired expenditures are smaller than total output. Given our present assumptions about the effects of a disequilibrium situation in the goods sector, the excess of saving over desired investment will tend to reduce the level of output (real income). The arrow pointing to the left at B in the centre panel represents this tendency.[1]

The initial forces generated in the disequilibrium situation discussed above have further repercussions on the whole system. The fall in the rate of interest generated by the excess supply of money in the money sector will affect desired investment, which we assumed to be a function of the rate of interest. The fall in the level of real income generated by the excess of saving over desired investment in the goods sector will affect the demand for money, which we assumed to be a function of real income. As the rate of interest falls desired investment rises, reducing the excess of saving over desired investment. As real income falls the demand for money and the rate of interest fall, strengthening the effects mentioned above. All of this will continue as long as either sector is in disequilibrium, ie until point A in figure 4.2 is reached.

This brief discussion of what is happening in the economy should be enough to point out why the *IS, LM* apparatus is so useful. It represents a very simple method of summarizing the assumptions we have been discussing, and the interrelationships

[1] Even though the *LM* curve is drawn for a particular price level (see the discussion at the end of chapter 3) the disequilibrium situation in the goods sector does not affect the *LM* curve. At this stage our assumptions about the goods sector are such that a disequilibrium situation there only affects the level of output, *not* the price level. Thus with our present assumptions the price level is not affected by any disequilibrium situation.

arising from these assumptions. It should also be clear that to understand what the *IS* and *LM* functions represent one has to understand the underlying economics, which as we saw can be quite complex even with the simple assumptions we have made so far.[1]

Now that we have examined the meaning of equilibrium in our two sectors it is useful to analyze how changes in behaviour of the participants will affect the two variables in which we are interested at present — the level of real income and the rate of interest. The four behavioural functions which are involved in determining equilibrium in the two sectors are the investment function, the consumption function, the demand for money function, and the supply of money function. These were the functions we used to derive the *IS* and the *LM* schedules, and therefore the behaviour represented by these functions is held constant along the *IS* and *LM* schedules. A shift in any of these functions (which represents a change in behaviour) will lead to a shift in the *IS* or *LM* sched le or both, and will result in a new equilibrium situation.

Let us start with a situation of overall equilibrium as shown by point *A* in figure 4.3. This is an equilibrium situation for that set of behavioural functions which underlies the derivation of the *IS* and *LM* schedules intersecting at *A*. Now let us assume that for some reason desired expenditures increase. For example, suppose there is a change in expectations about the future leading to a rise in desired investment at all interest rates (a shift in the investment function). Or because of changes in tastes desired consumptions at all income levels rises (a shift in the consumption function). These changes of behaviour can be represented by a shift of the *IS* schedule to the one marked *I'S'*. Now the economy is no longer in equilibrium at point *A*. It is true that with the level of real income and the rate of interest represented by point *A* the money sector is still in equilibrium — there has been no change in behaviour with respect to the allocation of wealth among money and bonds — but at point *A* the goods sector, now represented by *I'S'*, is no longer in equilibrium. Using the previous analysis we know that with the new *IS* schedule, point *A* represents a situation in which desired expenditures are greater than total output ($I > S$). This will lead to a rise in real income. As real income rises point *A* no longer represents equilibrium in the money sector either, because the rise in real income affects the quantity of money demanded and therefore the equilibrium in the money sector will also change, even though there has been no behavioural change in the money sector.[2] The rise in the interest rate will have further effects on desired investment and on the level of real income. This process will continue until a new equilibrium situation is reached at point *B* with real income at Y_B and the rate of interest at r_B. At this point both the money sector and the goods sector are again in

---

[1] It would be a useful exercise for the reader to trace out the forces generated at other possible disequilibrium points in figure 4.2.

[2] Because there has been no change in behaviour in the money sector the *LM* curve does not shift; the change in equilibrium is a movement along the curve.

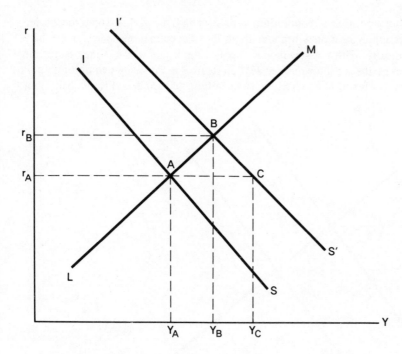

Figure 4.3

equilibrium. It should be noted here that if the shift in desired expenditures had not affected the rate of interest (via the effect of the change in real income on the demand for money), real income would have changed from Y_A to Y_C which is equal to the initial change in desired expenditures (consumption or investment) times the multiplier. The reason why real income only rises to Y_B is that some of the initial increase in desired expenditures is offset by the effect of the rise in the rate of interest on desired investment.

A shift of the *LM* schedule can occur because of a change in behaviour with respect to the demand for money, or because of a change in the supply of money.[1] An increase in the supply of money, or a decrease in the demand for money, can be represented by a shift of the *LM* schedule to the right.[2] To illustrate the effect of such changes let us

[1] A change in the real supply of money can arise either because of a change in the nominal quantity of money for given prices or because of a change in the price level for a given supply of nominal money.

[2] The reader should work out why this is so.

again start from a position of equilibrium at point A in figure 4.4. Assume there is an increase in the supply of money brought about by an open market operation by the monetary authority. With the new money supply equilibrium in the money sector can be represented by the schedule marked $L'M'$ in figure 4.4. At the old equilibrium point A the goods sector is still in equilibrium, since nothing has happened to the behaviour

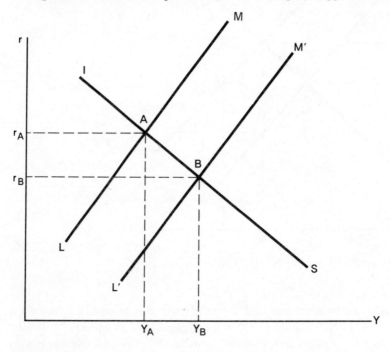

Figure 4.4

represented by the IS schedule. However, at point A and the new situation in the money sector represented by the $L'M'$ schedule, the quantity of money supplied is greater than the quantity of money demanded. Individuals will be attempting to re-allocate their wealth from money into bonds, thus driving the interest rate down. The fall in the interest rate also affects the goods sector via the effect of the rate of interest on desired investment; thus point A will not remain an equilibrium point for the goods sector either. The changes in the goods sector thus generated will have further repercussions on the money sector. The process will continue until a new equilibrium situation is reached at point B, at which both sectors are again in equilibrium.

The above discussion shows how changes in one sector of the economy are transmitted to the other sector, and how the final equilibrium of the whole system is the result of the interrelationship between the decisions about the allocation of wealth among alternative assets, and those about the allocation of goods among different uses. It is obvious that changes occurring in one sector can only be transmitted to another sector if there exist variables linking the two sectors, *and* if the changes affect these linking variables. In our discussion above, the linking variables were the rate of interest and the level of real income. The rate of interest was an effective linking variable, transmitting changes of behaviour occurring in the money sector to the goods sector, because the change in the money sector had an effect on the rate of interest, *and* the rate of interest entered into some decision in the goods sector, namely investment. Real income was an effective linking variable, transmitting changes of behaviour in the goods sector to the money sector, because the change in the goods sector had an effect on real income *and* real income entered into some decision in the money sector, namely the demand for money. To get a better grasp of these ideas, which play an important role in our later analysis, we shall look at some cases in which the linking variables are not effective in transmitting changes from one sector to another. We shall examine three cases: when the supply of money is perfectly elastic with respect to the interest rate; when the demand for money is perfectly elastic with respect to the interest rate; and when the desired investment function is perfectly inelastic with respect to the interest rate. We shall start with the most famous of these cases − the perfectly elastic demand for money or, as it is usually called, the case of the liquidity trap.[1]

When we discussed the theory of the demand for money we used the rate of interest as a measure of the alternative cost of holding wealth in the form of money rather than in the form of other assets, and thus a measure of the cost of acquiring the services yielded by money. When the rate of interest is zero, the cost of acquiring the services yielded by money is zero and we would expect that people would be willing to hold all their wealth in the form of money rather than other assets.

It is also possible that even when the rate of interest is positive the expected cost of holding wealth in the form of money is still zero. When we discussed the speculative motive for holding money (p. 28) we saw that one of the costs of holding bonds is the risk of a capital loss arising from a change in the rate of interest. If people expect a rise in the interest rate, ie a fall in the capital value of a bond, the expected return from holding a bond is equal to the interest yield less the expected capital loss. If these two are equal the expected return is zero, even though the interest yield is positive. In this situation the expected cost of holding money rather than bonds is zero. Assume for example that individuals become accustomed to some rate of interest which they then consider to be the 'normal' interest rate. Call this rate r_n. If the rate of interest falls below r_n individuals expect the rate of interest to rise back to r_n and therefore they

---

[1] This case was made famous by Keynes in his argument against the Classical economists. A detailed examination of that debate is presented in the appendix to chapter 5.

expect to suffer a capital loss if they hold bonds. Let r_L (less than r_n) be a rate of interest such that the capital loss which would occur if the rate of interest rises from r_L to the expected rate r_n exactly offsets the return represented by r_L. In this case, at an interest rate of r_L the expected return from holding a bond is zero, at an interest above r_L it is positive, at an interest rate below r_L it is negative. This situation can be represented by a demand curve for money which becomes perfectly elastic at the interest rate r_L.

Figure 4.5(a) shows four demand curves for money for four different levels of income, where $Y_1 < Y_2 < Y_3 < Y_4$, having the property that at an interest rate of r_L they become perfectly elastic – at this rate of interest people are willing to hold all their wealth in the form of money. M_1^s and M_2^s represent two different supply curves of money. In figure 4.5(b) we derive the LM curves representing this situation, which also have the property of being perfectly elastic at the interest rate r_L for the income levels up to Y_2 for LM_1 and up to Y_3 for LM_2. We can see that the change in the money

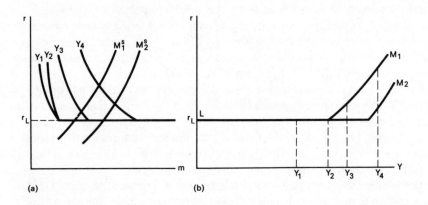

Figure 4.5

supply from M_1^s to M_2^s only affects that segment of the LM curve to the right of Y_2. The reason for this is that an increase in the supply of money along the perfectly elastic segment of the demand curve for money has no effect on the interest rate. Individuals are willing to hold more money, rather than bonds, at the given rate r_L. At this rate the cost of holding money is zero and individuals are indifferent between money and bonds.

Figure 4.6 represents a situation of general equilibrium for a goods sector represented by the IS curve shown, and a money sector exhibiting the properties discussed above, represented by LM_1, with equilibrium for both sectors on the horizontal part of the LM curve, at Y_e and r_L respectively. Assume there is now an increase in the supply of

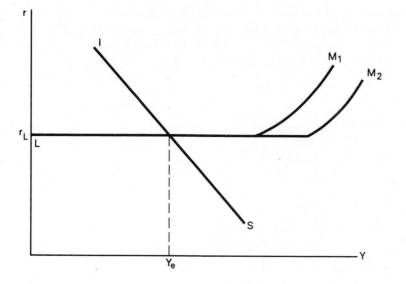

Figure 4.6

money shown by a shift of the *LM* curve from LM_1 to LM_2. As can be seen in figure 4.6 this has no effect on the equilibrium value of real income or the rate of interest because that part of the *LM* curve affected by this change is not relevant to the determination of equilibrium.[1]

A similar situation can occur if instead of the demand for money being perfectly elastic we have a situation where the supply of money is perfectly elastic. This can occur (and does quite frequently) when the monetary authority decides to fix the interest rate at some given level. To do this they have to be willing to supply whatever quantity of money is demanded at that rate otherwise the rate of interest would be affected by the excess demand or supply of money and could not be maintained at the desired level. This situation is shown in figure 4.7(a) which shows a supply curve that is perfectly elastic at an interest rate of r_f , and three demand curves for three income levels. In figure 4.7(b) we derive the *LM* curve for this situation which is perfectly elastic at an interest rate of r_f. We can see that any changes in the demand for money, for example a shift of all the demand curves to the right, will have no effect on the *LM* curve.[2]

[1] We can also see that a change in desired expenditures which shifts the *IS* curve along the horizontal part of the *LM* curve will change real income by the full multiplier effect. (Compare this with the case of an upward sloping *LM* curve discussed above).

[2] Changes in the price level will also have no effect on the *LM* curve in this situation.

If we combine the *LM* curve of figure 4.7(b) with an *IS* curve we will have the same situation as the one in figure 4.6 above (except that there will be no upward sloping part to the *LM* curve). Again, changes in the demand for money (or the price level) will have no effect on the equilibrium level of income or the rate of interest.

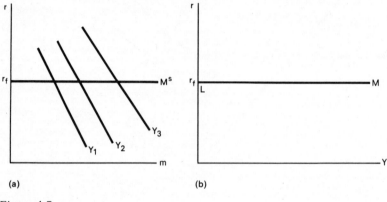

Figure 4.7

We now turn to the perfectly inelastic investment function. We recall that the *IS* curve represents all the combinations of income and the rate of interest at which desired expenditures equal total output. The reason why both the rate of interest and the level of real income are relevant here is that we assumed that both of these variables enter into the decisions about desired expenditures; the rate of interest for desired investment and real income for desired consumption. If we now drop the assumption that desired investment depends on the rate of interest, then real income becomes the only variable that affects desired expenditures, and the *IS* curve incorporating this assumption will be perfectly inelastic with respect to the rate of interest. Figure 4.8 shows such an *IS* curve with two *LM* curves representing two different conditions in the money sector (for example two different money supply functions). We can see that with both *LM* curves general equilibrium in the two sectors occurs at the same level of real income but at different interest rates. Thus any changes in the money sector (represented by shifts of the *LM* curve) only affect the rate of interest, and leave real income unchanged. However, changes in the goods sector (shifts of the *IS* curve) affect both real income and the rate of interest.

The three cases we have examined above are important in showing how, by varying certain assumptions about behaviour, we change the interrelationship between the goods and the money sectors. In the first two cases — the perfectly elastic demand for money, and the perfectly elastic supply of money — we still assumed that there was a linking variable between the money sector and the goods sector; desired investment

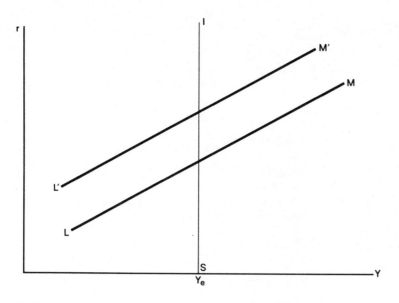

Figure 4.8

was assumed to be a function of the rate of interest. However, the assumptions about the money sector were such that any changes in that sector did not affect the linking variable — the rate of interest — and therefore changes were not transmitted into any changes in the goods sector. In the last case, the assumption of a perfectly inelastic investment function implies that the goods sector is totally independent of the money sector — no behaviour in the goods sector is affected by what happens in the money sector. Even though changes in the money sector affect the rate of interest, this is totally irrelevant to what happens in the goods sector because in this case the rate of interest plays no role in any behaviour relevant to the goods sector.[1] However, changes in the goods sector do affect the money sector because the variable linking the money sector to the goods sector — real income — is still operative as long as the demand for money is a function of the level of real income.

[1] It would be instructive for the reader to work out the implication of assuming that consumption itself is a function of the rate of interest also. This would reintroduce a link between the money and the goods sectors even though desired investment were not a function of the rate of interest.

references

HICKS J R 'Mr. Keynes and the Classics' in M G Mueller (ed.) *Readings in Macroeconomics.* Holt Rinehart and Winston 1966.
STEIN J L 'A Method of Identifying Disturbances which Produce Changes in Money National Income' *Journal of Political Economy* February 1960.

chapter 5

the output and employment sectors

In this chapter we shall fill the gap left in our previous analysis of the goods sector in chapters 2 and 4, and examine in more detail the determinants of real output – the flow of real goods and services produced by the economy per period time. Until now we assumed that the level of output depended only on the level of desired expenditures (aggregate demand). We did not specify any links by which changes in aggregate demand would be transmitted to changes in output. Suppliers of output were cast in a passive role, always reacting to the vagaries of aggregate demand, and suppliers of labour were treated in a similarly undignified manner. To get a more useful theory of the supply of output we first examine an employment sector in which we assume flexible wages (section 5.1), and then combine it with the other two sectors examined earlier (section 5.2). We then drop the assumption of flexible wages and examine the implication of a fixed money wage on the equilibrium of the economy (sections 5.3, 5.4). As soon as suppliers become active participants in determining the equilibrium level of output, the price level becomes an important equilibrating variable. We therefore present a more compact model of the determination of the price level (section 5.5) and use it to analyze some of the cases in which the linking variables are not operative (section 5.6). A schematic summary of the various models is then presented (section 5.7). In the appendix to this chapter we use the model to examine the controversy between Keynes and the Classics.

5.1 Employment and output with flexible wages
Given the state of technology in an economy, the level of output will depend on the quantity of labour and capital employed (where we assume that labour and capital are the only factors of production). We can express this relationship by a production function which relates the level of output to the level of inputs, for example, $Y = F(L, K)$ where L and K represent the quantity of labour and capital respectively, and Y the level of output (and real income). If we are mainly interested in analyzing short-run changes in the economy we can treat the stock of capital as being fixed (ie we can assume that investment – the change in the capital stock – is so small relative to the total stock that it can be ignored).[1] Thus we have $Y = F(L, K^{\bar{0}})$, where $K^{\bar{0}}$ is constant

[1] As we saw previously we cannot ignore the effect of investment on desired expenditures and

for short-run analysis or $Y = G\,(L)$, ie the level of output depends only on the quantity of labour employed, given the particular stock of capital K^0. This relation is shown graphically in figure 5.1.1, where we measure employment on the horizontal axis and output on the vertical axis. Given any level of employment the production function shows the level of output the economy will produce for some given stock of capital. But to determine what the level of employment will be we have to look at the labour market.[1]

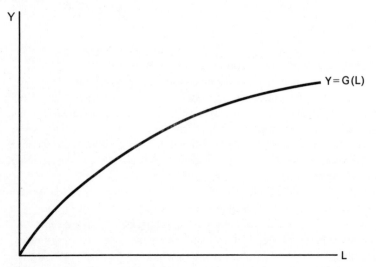

Figure 5.1.1

We shall define equilibrium in the labour market as the situation in which the quantity of labour demanded is equal to the quantity of labour supplied. As far as the demand for labour is concerned, we shall assume that firms in the economy will be willing to hire labour up to the point at which the real wage rate is equal to the marginal product of labour.[2] We can derive the marginal product curve of labour from the production function and, if we assume diminishing returns over the relevant range, the marginal product curve will be downward-sloping. Thus the demand curve for labour

via this on total output. Here we are talking about the effect of investment on the capital stock and via this on the potential output that can be produced by the economy.

[1] In our previous analysis, where we concentrated on aggregate demand, we implicitly assumed that the labour market reacted passively and provided exactly that level of employment which would satisfy aggregate demand.

[2] Here we assume competitive hiring of labour in the economy and profit-maximizing behaviour by firms.

will be the marginal product curve when plotted against the real wage rate, and will depend only on technology and the fixed stock of capital, K^o, assumed when deriving the production function. As far as the supply of labour is concerned we shall first assume that it is also a function of the real wage rate. We assume that when making the choice between work and leisure, individuals look at the real wage rate, because this shows the quantity of goods they can acquire for the leisure they give up. We also assume that the supply curve of labour is upward-sloping.[1]

The behavioural assumptions about the demand and the supply of labour are shown in figure 5.1.2(a) below. On the horizontal axis we measure the quantity of labour (L), and on the vertical axis the real wage rate (w). L^s is the supply curve, and L^d is the demand curve (this is the marginal product curve of labour derived from the production function reproduced in figure 5.1.2(b). We also assume that any disequilibrium situation in the labour market will affect the money wage rate and via this the real wage rate, and therefore the quantity of labour employed. The equilibrium real wage rate and employment rate will be w_f and L_f respectively. At any real wage rate above w_f there will be an excess supply of labour, forcing the wage rate down; at any real wage rate below w_f there will be an excess demand for labour, forcing the wage rate up.

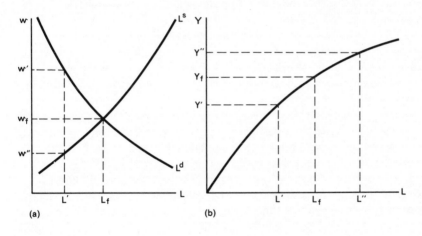

Figure 5.1.2

From the production function in figure 5.1.2(b) we can derive the level of output that will be produced by the economy for each level of employment. We can see that only one level of output, Y_f, corresponding to the level of employment, L_f, is

[1]This assumes that the substitution effect of a rise in the real wage rate (leisure is now more expensive) is stronger than the income effect of the rise in the wage rate.

consistent with equilibrium in the labour market. A lower level of output, say Y', corresponding to the level of employment L', implies *either* an excess supply of labour at the wage rate w', leading to a fall in the wage rate; *or* an excess demand for labour at the wage rate w'', leading to a rise in the wage rate. In both cases the change in the wage rate generated by the disequilibrium situation in the labour market will lead to a rise in employment and an increase in output. Any output greater than Y_f, say Y'' corresponding to employment L'', would imply that in the labour market either demanders or suppliers of labour were off their behavioural schedules.[1]

Before combining the output and employment sector with the other sectors studied earlier, it will be useful to understand how the introduction of this sector changes the whole structure of our model. We defined equilibrium in the goods sector as the situation in which the total output of the economy was equal to desired expenditures. Until now we assumed that if this were not so, total output would always adjust to desired expenditures by some means or other. Thus the answer to the question of what would happen if total output were not equal to desired expenditures was that total output would change. Such an answer implies that there are no *behavioural* relationships independent of desired expenditures, determining the supply of output. The introduction of the output and employment sector reverses this situation completely. Now we are saying that output is *behaviourally* determined by the supply of labour and technology. However, these are not necessarily related to desired expenditures. We can no longer say that if desired expenditures are not equal to output, output will change, unless we can show what variable is affected by the discrepancy between desired expenditures and output, and whether this variable is relevant to the behaviour determining the supply of output.

The possibility of a discrepancy between the level of output and desired expenditures not automatically eliminated by a change in output, means that we have to introduce some variable that will react to this new disequilibrium possibility. We therefore introduce the assumption that a discrepancy between the level of output and the level of desired expenditures will affect the price level. Whenever the level of output is greater than desired expenditures, prices will fall; whenever it is lower, prices will rise. We can now add the new sector — the employment sector — to our previous model of the economy.

5.2   General equilibrium with flexible wages
In figure 5.1.3 the *IS* and the *LM* curves summarize the conditions of equilibrium in

---

[1] This is different from the situation shown by the wage rate w' with employment at L' in figure 5.1.2(a). It is true that at w', L', suppliers of labour are not on their supply curve, but the situation is consistent with the supply curve which shows the maximum quantity they would be willing to supply. However, if employment were at L'' either suppliers or demanders of labour would be supplying or demanding more than the *maximum* amount they are willing to supply or demand.

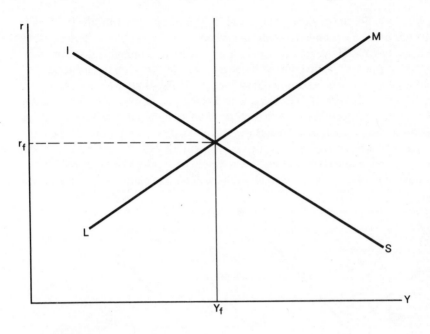

Figure 5.1.3

the money sectors and the goods sectors respectively. The Y_f line shows the one level
of output at which the employment sector will be in equilibrium — when the quantity
of labour demanded is equal to the quantity of labour supplied — and is derived from
the production function and the supply of labour function of figure 5.1.2 above. The
Y_f line is vertical because on our present assumptions the rate of interest plays no role
in the determination of equilibrium in the employment sector. Any point off the Y_f
line implies an excess demand or an excess supply of labour, which will lead to a change
in the real wage rate, employment, and output. For the whole economy to be in equilibrium we must have equilibrium in all the sectors. If any sector is not in equilibrium
some variable will change in that sector and this may affect the combination of real
income and the rate of interest at which all the three sectors are in equilibrium — desired
expenditures are equal to total output; the quantity of money demanded is equal to
the quantity of money supplied; and the quantity of labour demanded is equal to the
quantity of labour supplied.

To get a better understanding of equilibrium, let us examine the forces that will be
generated in the system in a disequilibrium situation, and how these forces operate to
bring the economy back to equilibrium. In figure 5.2.1 two possible disequilibrium
situations are shown. With the *IS* curve shown and the *L'M'* curve, the goods and money

sectors are in equilibrium at the point marked A. This means that with the particular combinations of variables underlying the derivation of these two curves desired expenditures are equal to Y_A. However, given the conditions in the employment sector, and the production function, actual output is equal to Y_f and there is thus an excess demand for goods and services approximately equal to $Y_A - Y_f$. Given our present assumptions about the effects of a discrepancy between desired expenditures and the level of output, the disequilibrium situation represented by point A will lead to a rise in prices. We can now use the analysis at the end of chapters 2 and 3 to see how this rise in prices will affect some or all of the variables entering the determination of equilibrium in the goods and money sectors, to see whether the price rise generated by the excess of desired expenditures over total output will tend to eliminate the disequilibrium situation.

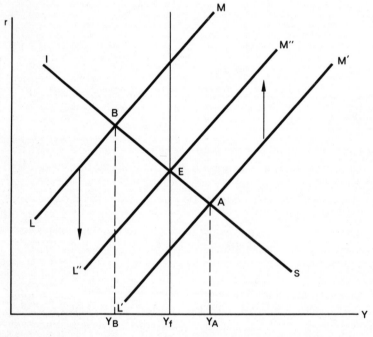

Figure 5.2.1

As far as the *IS* curve is concerned, we saw (p. 22) that changes in the price level have no effect on any of the variables entering into its construction. We assumed that the behaviour represented by the *IS* curve (desired consumption and desired investment) was not affected by the price level — it was all specified in real terms. As far as the money sector is concerned, we saw (p. 41) that changes in the price level did affect equilibrium in this sector, because even though the demand for money was specified (behaviourally) in real terms, the supply of money was in nominal terms. Thus the rise in the price level generated by the excess of desired expenditures over total output will lead to a fall in the real quantity of money in the economy. This is shown in figure 5.2.1 by the arrow from $L'M'$ which shows the direction of the shift in the LM curve due to the rise in prices. The rise in prices will continue as long as there is an excess of desired expenditures over total output, which means as long as the IS and LM curves intersect at a point to the right of E. When the real quantity of money is such that equilibrium in the money sector is represented by the $L''M''$ curve, all the sectors will again be in equilibrium. We see that the change in the price level eliminates the discrepancy between desired expenditures and the level of output by changing desired expenditures (from Y_A to Y_F). However, this does not occur directly. The change in the price level has a direct effect only on the real quantity of money in the economy. The change in desired expenditures occurs because of the link between the real quantity of money and the rate of interest *and* the link between the rate of interest and desired investment. These links are implicit in the IS and LM curves drawn in figure 5.2.1. It should be noted that the change in the price level has no effect on the Y_f curve, which shows equilibrium in the employment sector, because all the behavioural variables in that sector were specified in real terms — the real wage rate, and technology.[1]

Let us now examine the disequilibrium situation represented by point B in figure 5.2.1. Desired expenditures at point B equal Y_B. If the employment sector is in equilibrium the output of the economy is equal to Y_f, and point B represents a situation in which output is greater than desired expenditures. This discrepancy will lead to a fall in prices, and a rise in the real quantity of money (shown by a shift of the LM curve to the right), which will result in a fall in the rate of interest, and therefore a rise in desired investment. This process will continue as long as output is greater than desired expenditures ie until a new equilibrium situation is reached at E.

Another possibility at point B is that the goods sector is in equilibrium, desired expenditures and total output are equal to Y_B, but the employment sector is not. There is therefore no pressure on the price level. However, given the employment sector is in disequilibrium, something will have to change there. What sort of disequilibrium in the employment sector is implied by this situation? It might be thought that because desired expenditures and the level of output, at point B, are less than the full employment

---

[1] It is true that given any money wage rate a change in the price level will affect the real wage rate, but on our present assumptions any change in the real wage rate, due to a change in the price level, will be offset by a change in the money wage rate. One can see this clearly in figure 5.1.2(a) above. Assume that for some given money wage rate and price level the real wage rate is w_f. Now assume that the price level rises so that the real wage rate falls to w''. At this point there is an excess demand for labour driving the money wage rate up until the real wage rate is again w_f. Only at this real wage is the labour market in equilibrium.

level of output, this situation implies an excess supply of labour. But this is clearly wrong. All we know is that at point *B* employment is less than the full employment level. This can occur either because the real wage rate is too high and there is an excess supply of labour or because the real wage rate is too low and there is an excess demand for labour (see p. 61). On our present assumptions about the employment sector the wage rate will fall if there is an excess supply of labour and rise if there is an excess demand for labour. In both cases employment and output will increase. However, as output increases a discrepancy is introduced between output and desired expenditures; prices will start falling, the real quantity of money will start rising and desired expenditures will start rising. This process will continue until we again have equilibrium in all the sectors at point *E*.

In figure 5.2.2 we can see the two possibilities just discussed and their implications for the forces generated in the system. The top right quadrant summarizes all the sectors of the economy — the *IS, LM* and Y_f curves. The bottom right quadrant shows the production function relating the level of output to the level of employment, and the bottom left quadrant represents the labour market (these two are reproductions on different axes of figure 5.1.2 above). The two possible types of disequilibrium situations

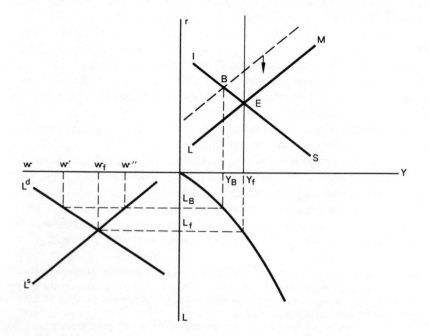

Figure 5.2.2

represented by point B depend on whether the actual employment at point B is L_f or L_B. If employment is L_f the labour market is in equilibrium and output is Y_f. This means that in the goods market desired expenditures (equal to Y_B) are less than actual output. All prices fall, and given the nominal stock of money, the real quantity of money rises, thus leading to a rise in desired investment via the change in the rate of interest. This is shown by a shift in the LM curve in the direction of the arrow. This process continues until all the markets are again in equilibrium at E. Real wages do not change – money wages change in the same proportion as the change in prices.

If the level of employment is L_B and therefore the level of actual output is Y_B, then point B represents equilibrium in the goods market – desired expenditures are equal to actual output – but disequilibrium in the labour market. Either the real wage rate is too high (w') and there is an excess supply of labour, or it is too low (w'') and there is an excess demand for labour. In the former case the money wage rate will fall (and therefore the real wage rate), in the latter case it will rise, and in both cases employment and output will increase. The increase in output means that the equilibrium situation in the goods market no longer holds; desired expenditures are now less than total output and this leads to a fall in prices and an increase in desired expenditures. This process continues until all markets are again in equilibrium at point E. Real wages rise or fall (depending on whether the initial situation was one of excess demand or excess supply), implying that money wages do not change in the same proportion as prices.

We can see from the above description that the two variables playing a crucial role in equilibrating the whole system are the wage rate and the price level. Changes in the wage rate caused by an excess supply of or demand for labour produce equilibrium in the employment sector, changes in the price level caused by an excess demand or supply of goods produce equilibrium in the goods sector. It is clear from the above description of the equilibrating process that wages and prices have to be flexible to be effective in performing the function of equilibrating the system. They have to react to a disequilibrium situation – wages in the labour market, and prices in the goods market. Moreover, the links by which changes in these two variables affect desired expenditures and the level of output have to be operative. If, for example, a disequilibrium in the goods market affects the price level but conditions in the money sector are such that changes in the price level do not affect the rate of interest and therefore have no effect on desired investment (see p. 55), then the price level does not affect desired expenditures and cannot act as the variable which eliminates the discrepancy between desired expenditures and the level of output. This situation is shown in figure 5.2.3, where we assume that the money sector has the properties that will lead to a perfectly elastic LM curve.

With flexible wages in the employment sector, total output will always be Y_f, otherwise the wage rate will change. The situation represented by figure 5.2.3 is thus

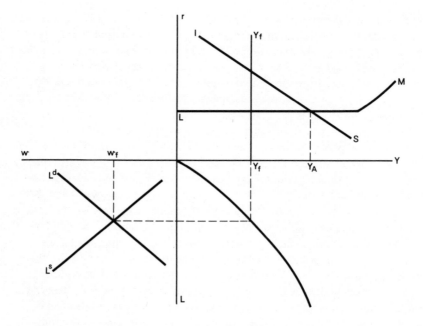

Figure 5.2.3

one in which desired expenditures (Y_A) are greater than total output, Y_f, therefore prices will start rising as before. However, the rise in prices has no effect on the disequilibrium situation. As far as the employment sector is concerned, the rise in prices has no effect on the quantity employed, because when the employment sector is in equilibrium money wages change at the same rate as prices, therefore real wages remain the same and therefore employment and output remain the same. As far as desired expenditures are concerned, the rise in prices also has no effect; it does not affect the *LM* curve in the relevant range. Thus we see that even though the disequilibrium situation in the goods market results in changes in the price level, these changes cannot eliminate the disequilibrium situation because the conditions in the money sector are such that the link between the price level and desired expenditures has been broken.

5.3   Fixed money wages
So far we have considered a situation in which the employment sector will always tend to full employment equilibrium – any excess supply or demand for labour will be eliminated by a change in the wage rate – and therefore the equilibrium level of output depends *only* on technology and the supply of labour. This assumption implies that the money wage rate can change when there is an excess demand or supply of labour;

it is only via changes in the money wage rate that a disequilibrium situation in the employment sector affects the real wage rate. We shall now drop this assumption and assume instead that the money wage rate is not flexible downwards. We still assume that the maximum quantity of labour supplied depends on the real wage rate, but we add to this the assumption that no labour will be supplied below some fixed money wage rate. The situation in the labour market with these assumptions is shown in figure 5.3.1(a).

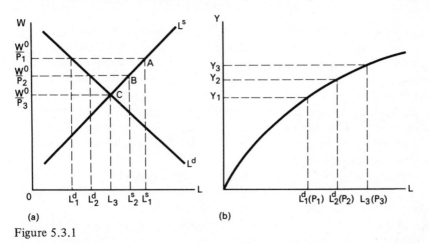

Figure 5.3.1

On the horizontal axis we measure the quantity of labour, and on the vertical axis the real wage rate, for some fixed money wage rate W^o and various price levels, where $P_1 < P_2 < P_3$. The demand curve for labour (L^d) is still a function of the real wage rate as before but now, because of the assumption that at any money wage rate below W^o no labour will be supplied, we have different supply curves of labour for different price levels. When the price level is P_1 the real wage rate is $\frac{W_o}{P_1}$. The maximum amount of labour supplied at this real wage is shown by the curve L^s and equals L_1^s. However, we have also assumed that at any money wage rate below W_o no labour will be supplied. Given the price level P_1 this assumption, translated into real wages, means that at any real wage below $\frac{W_o}{P_1}$ no labour will be supplied. Thus for the price level P_1 the supply curve for labour is $0 \frac{W^o}{P_1} AL^s$. Now assume the price level is $P_2 > P_1$. With the same fixed money wage rate W_o, the maximum amount of labour supplied will be L_2^s. However, for the price level P_2 the assumption that no labour will be supplied at a money wage rate less than W^o, means that no labour will be supplied at a real wage rate below $\dfrac{W^o}{P_2}$. Thus for P_2 the supply curve of labour is $0 \dfrac{W^o}{P_2} BL^s$. Similarly for other price levels.[1]

Let us now define equilibrium in a labour market in which the money wage rate is fixed. In figure 5.3.1(a) assume we are in the situation in which the fixed money wage is W^o and the price level is P_1, thus the real wage rate is $\dfrac{W^o}{P_1}$. At this real wage rate the quantity of labour demanded is L_1^d, the maximum quantity of labour supplied is L_1^s. There is thus an excess supply of labour. However, given our present assumption that the money wage rate is not flexible downwards, this excess supply of labour has no effect on the wage rate and therefore the level of employment. For the given money wage rate W^o and the price level P_1 the labour market is in 'equilibrium' with employment at L_1^d. Similarly for the given money wage rage W^o and a price level of P_2 the labour market is in 'equilibrium' with employment at L_2^d. We can see that once we introduce a fixed money wage rate the level of employment becomes a function of the fixed money wage rate *and* the price level.

Figure 5.3.1(b) shows a production function relating the level of output and the 'equilibrium' levels of employment for various price levels and the *given* fixed money wage rate of W^o. For example, when the price level is P_1 the equilibrium level of employment is L_1^d and the corresponding level of output is Y_1. Similarly for the other price levels. Now there is no longer a single level of output corresponding to equilibrium in the labour market, but many levels of output depending on the price level. The crucial difference resulting from the introduction of a fixed money wage rate into the labour market is that now the price level affects the equilibrium level of employment and therefore the equilibrium level of output (compare this with the analysis of figure 5.1.2 above).

5.4   General equilibrium with a fixed money wage rate

In figure 5.4.1 we combine the employment sector with the above characteristics with the rest of the economy. The axes in figure 5.4.1 are the same as those of figure 5.2.2 except that the real wage rate is now measured by $\dfrac{W^o}{P}$ where W^o is the assumed fixed money wage rate. Let us look at the situation at point B on the assumption that the LM curve passing through this point represents equilibrium in the money sector for the price level P_B. Thus desired expenditures at P_B are equal to Y_B. With the money wage

---

[1] If the fixed money wage rate is changed all the horizontal segments of the supply curves of labour also change. It is a useful exercise for the student to work out what would happen to the supply curves if the fixed money wage rate were cut to $W' < W^o$.

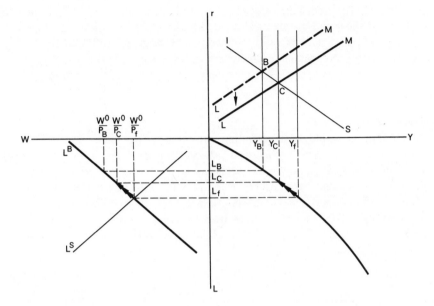

Figure 5.4.1

rate fixed at W^o and the price level P_B, the real wage rate is equal to $\dfrac{W^o}{P_B}$, and the levels

of employment and output are equal to L_B and Y_B respectively. The level of output is equal to desired expenditures and both the goods sector and the employment sector are in equilibrium; the excess supply of labour has no effect on employment and output and therefore on the equilibrium situation.

Let us now assume that the *LM* curve passing through point *B* represents equilibrium in the money sector for the price level P_f. At the fixed money wage rate W^o and the

price level P_f the real wage rate is $\dfrac{W^o}{P_f}$, the level of employment L_f and the level of out-

put Y_f. Thus the level of output is greater than desired expenditures. The discrepancy between the level of output and desired expenditures will lead to a fall in prices, an increase in the real quantity of money, a fall in the rate of interest and therefore an increase in desired expenditures (this is shown by a shift in the *LM* curve to the right). However, the fall in prices also raises the real wage rate, and therefore the levels of employment and output fall (the arrows on the demand curve for labour and the production function). This process will continue as long as there is an excess of output over desired expenditures ie until point *C* is reached with the price level at P_c. At this point desired expenditures and total output are equal to Y_C, and all the sectors are again in equilibrium. The crucial difference between the effects of the disequilibrium situation examined above and the identical disequilibrium situation examined in figure 5.2.2 previously, where we did not assume a fixed money wage rate, is that there, changes in prices were accompanied by changes in wages, keeping the real wage rate and therefore output constant at the given level associated with equilibrium in the labour market.

5.5   The price level

The introduction of the employment sector into our model of the economy, whether with flexible wages or a fixed money wage rate, shows the importance of the price level in achieving overall equilibrium in the economy; in both cases because of its effect on desired expenditures, and in the latter case because of its effect on the level of output also. It is therefore important to understand exactly how the price level is determined, and what real variables are affected by it. Even though the answer to these questions has been given in various places throughout this chapter it may be useful to summarize the results in a more compact way.

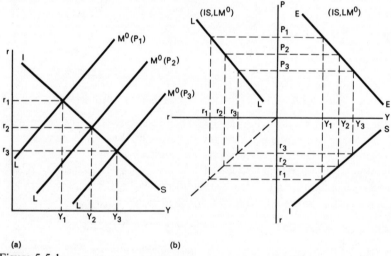

(a)   (b)

Figure 5.5.1

Figure 5.5.1(a) shows various equilibrium situations in the goods sector for a given *IS* curve (some specific consumption and investment function), and a given quantity of nominal money M^o at various price levels $P_1 > P_2 > P_3$. We can see that there is a unique relationship between the price level, the interest rate and the level of desired expenditures. This relationship is translated in figure 5.5.1(b) where the relationship between the price level and the level of real income is measured in the top right quadrant (the *EE* curve), and the relationship between the price level and the interest rate in the top left quadrant (the *LL* curve). Both of these curves are drawn for the assumed conditions in the goods and the money sectors shown in figure 5.5.1(a). A shift in the *IS* curve or the demand curve for money or the supply of nominal money will shift *both* of these curves. In the bottom right quadrant the *IS* curve from figure 5.5.1(a) is reproduced and the left quadrant has just a 45° line.

We now turn to the relationship between the price level and aggregate supply. We know from our previous analysis that whether aggregate supply is related to the price level depends on the conditions in the labour market, ie whether the wage rate is flexible or not. If the wage rate is flexible then the level of employment is uniquely determined independently of the price level and therefore aggregate supply is independent of the price level. If, however, the money wage rate is fixed the levels of employment and output become functions of the price level. These relationships are shown in figure 5.5.2.

The bottom two quadrants in figure 5.5.2 represent the labour market (left quadrant) and the production function (right quadrant) respectively. The top left quadrant shows

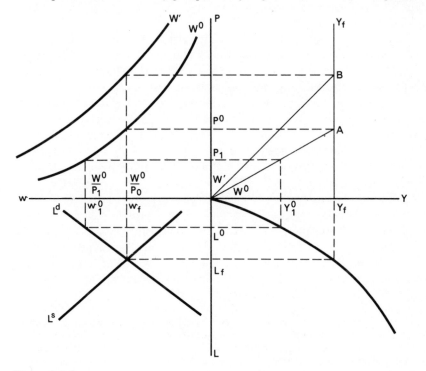

Figure 5.5.2

the relationship between the real wage rate (w) and the price level (P) for some given money wage rate. Thus the curve marked W^o shows the relationship between the price level and the real wage ($w = \dfrac{W^o}{P}$) when the money wage is fixed at W^o. Similarly with the curve marked W' which represents a money wage rate greater than W^o. We want to derive the relationship between aggregate supply and the price level in the top right quadrant. If the money wage rate is flexible we can ignore the top left quadrant, because in that case the equilibrium real wage will always be w_f, and employment and output will be L_f and Y_f respectively, whatever the price level. With flexible money wages aggregate supply is independent of the price level and is represented by the curve marked Y_fY_f. Assume now that the money wage is fixed at W^o. If the price level is P^o, the real wage rate is $\dfrac{W^o}{P^o} = w_f$, employment is L_f and output is Y_f. If the price level is P_1 the real wage rate is w_1^o, employment is L^o, and output is Y_1^o. If we do this for all price levels we get the curve marked W^oAY_f showing the relationship between output and the price level.[1] If the money wage rate is fixed at $W' > W^o$ then by the same procedure, the relationship between output and the price level is shown by the curve marked $W'BY_f$.

We can now combine figure 5.5.1(b) and the top right quadrant of figure 5.5.2 to see the interaction between desired expenditures and the level of output; this is done in figure 5.5.3 for flexible wages and 5.5.4 for fixed wages. If we have flexible wages the output sector is represented by the Y_fY_f curve and desired expenditures by the EE curve, for the IS curve shown and a quantity of nominal money represented by M^o. Equilibrium in the economy occurs at the output level Y_f, a price level P_f, and the interest rate r_f. At any price level above P_f the level of output will be greater than aggregate demand, driving prices down; at any price level below P_f desired expenditures will be greater than output, driving prices up. If now the quantity of money changes to $M' > M^o$ a shift of LL to $L'L'$, and of EE to $E'E'$ the new equilibrium in the economy will occur at an income level Y_f, an interest rate r_f and a price level P'. The only effect of the change in the quantity of money is to change the equilibrium price level; nothing real in the economy is affected. The equilibrium rate of interest and the equilibrium level of income are determined independently of what happens in the money sector. We see that for any given behaviour with respect to desired consumption and investment (ie for any given IS curve) the money sector (summarized by the LM

---

[1] We are assuming that the money wage rate is fixed downwards but not upwards, ie it cannot fall below W^o but it can rise above it. If the money wage rate were fixed in both directions then at prices above P_o employment and output would fall; we would be moving along the supply curve of labour. We are assuming, however, that an excess demand for labour will lead to a rise in the money wage rate even though an excess supply of labour will not lead to a fall in it.

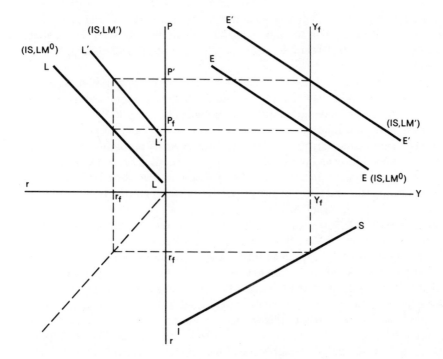

Figure 5.5.3

curve) *only* affects the price level. The above result may seem strange at first sight. When we analyzed the money sector we saw that the rate of interest was the equilibrating variable there, reacting to any excess demand or supply of money, yet when we put together the money sector with the rest of the economy now, we find that the equilibrium rate of interest is not affected by anything that may happen in the money sector.

The explanation of this seeming paradox is not hard to find. Once we introduce an independent determinant of the level of output, ie an employment sector with flexible wages, and we assume that prices are flexible, then the price level will always react to a disequilibrium between desired expenditures and the level of output via its effects on the real quantity of money, thus on the rate of interest and on desired expenditures. If the rate of interest is not at that level which makes desired expenditures equal to output (determined by the conditions in the employment sector) then the price level will change, thus changing the rate of interest. Only one interest rate (r_f in figure 5.5.3) is compatible with equilibrium between desired expenditures and the given level of output and this interest rate will be achieved by changes in the price level. Thus what we have now is that starting from an equilibrium situation in the economy, for example

Y_f, r_f, and P_f in figure 5.5.3, any change in the money sector will initially affect the interest rate as before, but this will have repercussions on the price level via the effect of the interest rate on the level of desired expenditures, and this will offset the initial effect on the interest rate.

So far we have examined the price level in a situation in which wages are flexible and therefore output is independent of the price level. If the money wage rate is fixed at W^o in figure 5.5.4 the relevant output curve is the one marked $W^o Y_f$. With the EE curve shown, general equilibrium in the economy will occur at an income level Y^o, price level P^o and interest rate r^o. At any price level above P^o output will be greater than desired expenditures and prices will fall, increasing desired expenditures via the effect on the interest rate, and decreasing the level of output via the effect on the real wage rate; the opposite will occur at any price level below P^o. If the fixed money wage were to rise to W' the new equilibrium situation would be one with a lower real income, a higher price level and a higher interest rate (Y', P', r'). Thus besides all the factors that were previously relevant in determining the price level, we now have another one – the fixed money wage. This is not surprising. The fixed money wage rate affects the level of output and it is the interaction between the level of output and desired expenditures that determines the price level. A change in the money sector, for example an increase in the quantity of money from M^o to M' will shift the EE curve to $E'E'$ and the LL curve to $L'L'$. The effect of this will be to raise the level of income to Y'', the price level to P'', and to lower the rate of interest to r''.[1] In this case changes in the money sector do affect the rate of interest and the price level. The difference between this case and the previous one with flexible wages is that now the initial effect of the change in the money sector of increasing desired expenditures, and therefore the price level, is accompanied by a change in the level of output. Thus the disequilibrium created between desired expenditures and the level of output is 'eliminated' both by a decrease in desired expenditures due to the rise in prices *and* an increase in output due to the rise in prices; in the previous case only the former occurred.

5.6   The extreme cases
We can use the above analysis to examine the effects on the equilibrium of the economy when the links between the money sector and the goods sector are broken, either

---

[1] In both this case and the previous ones changes in desired expenditures can be similarly analyzed. An increase in desired expenditures shown by a shift in the *IS* curve will also shift the *LL* and *EE* curves upwards. The effects of this on income and prices will be the same as those due to an increase in the quantity of money, examined above; however, the effect on the interest rate may be different. It is a useful exercise for the reader to carry out such an analysis and understand the economic meaning of the results he gets. For example, why, in the flexible wages case, does an increase in desired expenditures due to a shift in the consumption function affect the interest rate, but one due to an increase in the quantity of money affect *only* prices?

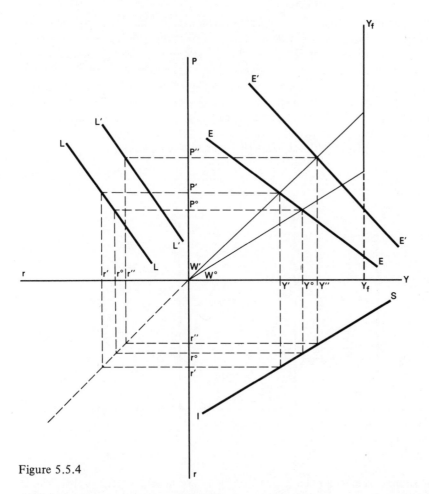

Figure 5.5.4

because the *LM* curve is perfectly elastic (a perfectly elastic supply or demand for money), or because of a perfectly inelastic *IS* curve. In terms of figure 5.5.3 both of these would lead to a perfectly inelastic *EE* curve, but the *LL* curve would be different, depending on whether the *LM* curve were perfectly elastic or the *IS* curve perfectly inelastic; in the former case the *LL* curve would be perfectly inelastic, in the latter it would be upward-sloping.[1] In figure 5.6.1 we show a situation in which the money sector is characterized by a perfectly elastic *LM* curve. The axes and the meaning of the

[1] It would be a useful exercise for the student to check these statements by deriving the relevant *EE* and *LL* curves from the appropriate *IS* and *LM* curves.

curves are the same as those of the top part of figure 5.5.4. First, let us assume that the employment sector is one with flexible wages, therefore the $Y_f Y_f$ curve is the one representing the output sector. With the *EE* curve as drawn we see that desired expenditures at *any* price level are Y_E and the level of output at any price level is Y_f. The excess of output over desired expenditures will drive prices down, but with our present assumptions this has no effect on any of the variables in the system. There is no way by which equilibrium can be achieved. If the *EE* curve cuts the Y axis to the right of the $Y_f Y_f$ curve the opposite would be true; prices would start rising and continue to do so without any effect on the system. This is the case we examined in figure 5.2.3 above.

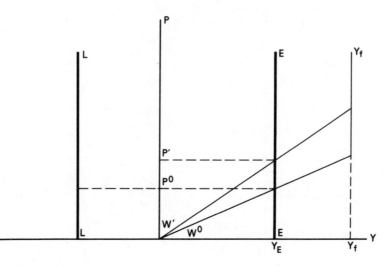

Figure 5.6.1

If the employment sector is characterized by a fixed money wage rate of W^0 the output sector is shown by the $W^0 Y_f$ curve. With the *EE* curve as shown, equilibrium in the economy will occur at a price level of P^0. At any price level above P^0 output would be greater than desired expenditures and the price level would fall, raising real wages and thus reducing the level of employment and output. A rise of the fixed money wage rate to W' would raise the price level by the same amount (to P'), leaving the real wage rate, the level of employment and output unchanged. This is a situation in which the price level can still operate to equilibrate the economy, even though it has no effect on desired expenditures, by its effect on the level of output. If the *EE* curve intersected the Y axis to the right of the $Y_f Y_f$ curve we would have the same situation as in the case of flexible wages. The price level would rise and continue to rise indefinitely, with the level of output remaining at Y_f.

5.7   Summary

In the last six sections we analyzed three different models of an economy and traced out the implications of these on the interrelationships among the different types of economic decision-making, and on the forces generated within the economy when changes occur in some sector. We saw that different assumptions can lead to quite different implications about how the economic system works. The differences arise mainly because the different assumptions imply different types of links transmitting the effects of changes among the variables. Even though it is true that in a general equilibrium system 'everything depends on everything else' it is important to understand why this is so, and how this dependence is itself a function of particular *economic* assumptions.

To highlight the important concepts that we have used in the models so far examined, it will be useful to summarize the models in a less formal way, not with an aim of drawing any further implications from them but to bring out the substantive economic differences among them.

The three models are presented schematically in table 5.7.1. Model 1 is the one presented in chapter 4, in which only desired expenditures play a role in determining real income. Model 2 is the one which incorporates an employment sector with flexible wages, and model 3 an employment sector with a fixed money wage rate. The three sectors whose interrelationship is to be examined are the money sector, the goods sector, and the employment sector — the columns in the table. The circled variables in the table are the assumed equilibrating variables for the market in question, the arrows linking the variables are the assumed relationships among the variables.

Model 1 is a very simple one, but even here the idea of the links among the sectors leads to quite a complicated relationship. The money sector is represented by some demand curve for real money (m^d), a fixed supply of nominal money M^s, which, given the price level (P), represents a supply of real money of $\dfrac{M^s}{P}$. The price level does not appear anywhere else in the model. It is exogenous, affecting some variables, but not affected by any, in the model. The goods sector is represented by two types of desired expenditures, C and I, which determine total desired expenditures Y_e, which in turn determines total output Y_o, and employment L which will be whatever is necessary to produce Y_e. In this model we did not specify any variable linking desired expenditures and the levels of output and employment; the latter two always adjust to whatever is necessary to make output equal to desired expenditures. Within the goods sector there is also a link running from Y_e to C, which represents the assumption that desired consumption depends on the level of income, and hence there is a two-way link between C and Y_e (the two-way arrow). It is exactly because of this two-way relationship that we were led to the multiplier analysis of chapter 2. There are two links between the

Table 5.7.1

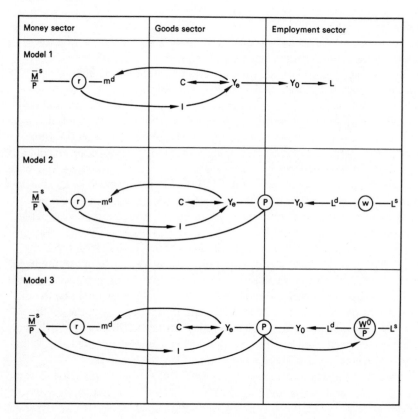

money sector and the goods sector; one between m^d and Y_e because of the assumption that the demand for money is a function of income, and one between r and I because of the assumption that investment is a function of the rate of interest. It is these two links that made the goods sector dependent both on the level of income and the rate of interest — the whole *IS, LM* analysis. We can see clearly from this — merely schematic — representation that, for example, changes in income will also affect the level of investment, not because of any behavioural relationship between the two but because of the links between income and the money sector, and between the money sector and investment.

   We can also easily see the meaning of some of the extreme cases examined at the end of chapter 4. For example we saw there (p. 56) that if we dropped the assumption that investment is a function of the rate of interest, the *IS* curve would be perfectly inelastic, implying that changes in the money sector would not affect real income. From the schematic representation of model 1 we can see that the only link between the money sector and the goods sector operates through the rate of interest and investment; it is not surprising therefore that when this link is cut there is no way by which events in the money sector can be transmitted to the goods sector.

From the schematic representation of model 2, we can see how the introduction of an employment sector with flexible wages crucially changes the linkages among the sectors. The equilibrium level of output no longer depends on aggregate demand, but is uniquely determined by the supply of labour, and the demand for labour (which itself depends on the production function). Given that aggregate demand and the level of output now depend on different variables, we introduced the price level as the equilibrating variable between the two. Thus in this model the price level is endogenous, being determined within the model. We can also see that the link by which the price level acts to equilibrate any discrepancy between aggregate demand and the level of output works through the money sector. For this to be an effective equilibrating mechanism there must also exist a link between the money sector and the goods sector. If there is no link between the money sector and the goods sector, perhaps because investment is not a function of the rate of interest, then the price level, even though it affects the money sector, will not affect aggregate demand, and will therefore not be able to act as an equilibrating variable between aggregate demand and the level of output. This is the case we examined in figure 5.2.3 above.

When we fix the money wage rate (W^o) in model 3, we add another link to the system. Now the level of output depends not only on the demand and supply of labour, but also on the fixed money wage rate and the price level. The price level now links aggregate demand and the level of output by converting into real terms the two nominal variables exogenously given: the nominal quantity of money and the fixed money wage rate.

5.8   Appendix

In this appendix we use the framework of analysis developed in the chapter to examine the debate which, at least in the textbook literature, has become known as 'Keynes versus the Classics'. The Classical economists[1] maintained two propositions about the equilibrium properties of an economy with flexible wages and prices. First, that the equilibrium is one with full employment of labour. Second, that the nominal quantity of money in the economy only determines the equilibrium price level, but has no effect on the equilibrium value of any real variable. A real variable is one which has an effect

---

[1] I an using the term 'Classical economists' rather loosely. In this context it refers to the development of the Classical tradition by Thornton, Wicksell, Pigou and Marshall, as it more or less existed at the time of Keynes.

on the allocation of resources either at a point of time or over time. For example, the relative prices of commodities affect the quantities of commodities produced and consumed at a point of time; the interest rate affects the quantities of commodities consumed over time. In the present context the real variables in which we are interested are real income, the real wage rate and the interest rate. According to the second Classical proposition none of these variables are determined by the nominal quantity of money in the economy; their equilibrium values depend only on real factors — tastes, technology, and the quantity of resources in the economy.[1]

In the first model presented in this chapter (sections 5.1 and 5.2) both Classical propositions hold. Wage flexibility results in a full employment equilibrium in the labour market, and price flexibility results in the equality between the aggregate supply and demand for goods at the full employment level of output. In this model it is also true that the rate of interest is not affected by the nominal quantity of money. Given tastes, technology, and the quantity of resources in the economy, all real variables are determined; the nominal quantity of money only determines the price level. To understand the debate centering around the two Classical propositions it is important to understand how price flexibility results in full employment equilibrium, and what role the nominal quantity of money plays in the process. As we shall see what is crucial is not price flexibility as such, but interest rate flexibility. With a given nominal stock of money, price flexibility is the means by which the interest rate changes to its equilibrium value which is determined by real factors.

In figure 5.8.1 we start with a situation of full employment equilibrium at Y_f, r_f, for some price level P_o. r_f is the real rate of interest, the rate at which full employment saving is equal to investment. Assume now that there is a change in tastes, say, and everybody decides they want to save more than previously. This can be shown by a shift of the IS curve to the one marked $I'S'$. The new equilibrium interest rate should be r'_f, at which point the new level of saving at full employment will again be equal to investment. However, if there is no change in the price level the rate of interest will only fall to r_m and in this case aggregate demand will be Y_m, less than the full employment level of output Y_f.

To attain the new full employment equilibrium the rate of interest has to fall, and investment has to rise. The reason for this is clear. People desire to save more than previously, they want more future consumption relative to current consumption. To provide more future consumption investment has to increase. A change in the interest rate is the signalling device transmitting the information about the change in tastes (between present and future consumption), and providing the incentive to act on this information (to increase investment). However, the direct effect of the change in

---

[1] Tastes affect the choices among present consumption, future consumption and leisure, ie, consumption, saving, and the supply of labour.

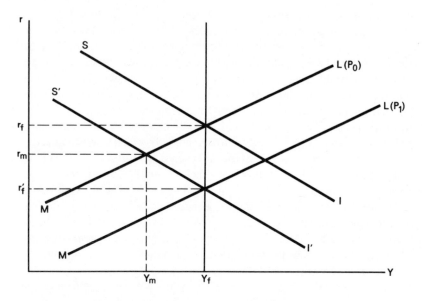

Figure 5.8.1

saving is on the price level. What about the interest rate?

With a given nominal quantity of money the fall in the price level leads to an increase in the real quantity of money, and thereby a fall in the interest rate. As long as there is an excess supply of goods, an excess of saving over investment, the price level and there-fore the interest rate will continue falling. Once the interest rate reaches r_f' (when the price level is P_1) full employment saving is again equal to investment, and we have the new equilibrium. We can see from the above description that what is crucial to the first Classical proposition is the flexibility of the interest rate. If the rate of interest can not fall, for some reason or another, flexibility of prices will not be enough to attain full employment.

In the above model we can see that the second Classical proposition also holds. A change in the nominal quantity of money, without a change in any real factors, will only affect the price level. Any initial effect on the interest rate will be offset by the change in the price level induced by the excess supply or demand for goods.[1]

Keynes' argument against the first Classical proposition was essentially a very simple one.[2] The Classical proposition requires that the rate of interest be flexible; it is the

[1] See the discussion pp. 75-76.

[2] For a discussion of the second Classical proposition see L.A. Metzler, 'Wealth, Saving, and the Rate of Interest', *Journal of Political Economy*, April 1951.

essential link between saving decisions and investment decisions. The question is therefore whether price and wage flexibility guarantee the necessary interest rate flexibility? Keynes argued that in a money economy there existed an inherent inflexibility in the interest rate whatever is the flexibility in wages and prices, namely, the rate of interest in a money economy could never fall below zero.[1] In figure 5.8.2 we start again with a situation of full employment equilibrium at Y_f and r_f. Assume, as previously, that because of a change in tastes people want to save more at every level of income, shown by the shift of the *IS* curve to the one marked $I'S'_1$. The new equilibrium rate of interest at which full employment saving is equal to investment is r'_f, which is less than zero. However, in a money economy the rate of interest cannot fall below zero. It would never pay on individual to lend someone £100 today say, on the promise to receive £90 at the end of the year; by not lending it he could have the full £100 instead.[2] Thus in the situation depicted in figure 5.8.2 there is an excess of full employment saving over investment, which will result in a fall of the price level, but this will not lead to a fall in the interest rate to the required level. Flexibility of prices in this case does not imply the necessary flexibility of the interest rate. In a money economy we have the ultimate liquidity trap at a zero rate of interest.

The rebuttal to Keyenes' criticism was made by Pigou[3] and has become enshrined in the literature under the title of the 'Pigou effect'. The power of the rebuttal is often underestimated because it is usually presented as an *ad hoc* solution to the problem raised by Keynes. Whereas in fact, as we shall see, it is a solution implied by the criticism itself. Let us first look at the mechanics of the solution.

Any discrepancy between full employment saving and investment can be eliminated either by a change in saving or a change in investment. Price flexibility can achieve a change in investment of the correct amount as long as it can affect the rate of interest by the correct amount. Keynes' point was that there may be a situation where price flexibility cannot do so; the rate of interest cannot fall by the required amount and therefore investment cannot rise by the required amount. However, another way of eliminating the discrepancy between saving and investment, is by a change in saving. The question is therefore whether price flexibility can do this? If consumption is solely a function of income, then a fall in the price level has no effect on consumption and therefore on saving. One has to rely on the investment side to solve the discrepancy between saving and investment. However, if consumption also depends on wealth, then

---

[1] This is Keynes' liquidity trap argument. Even though the liquidity trap can occur at a positive interest rate when the interest rate is expected to rise, the expected yield at that rate is zero. See pp.

[2] In a barter economy one might be willing to lend someone 100 bushels of wheat say, on the promise of receiving 90 bushels at the end of the year, because there might be costs in holding the 100 bushels oneself. For example, mice might eat 20 bushels over the year and one would be worse off by not lending at the negative interest rate.

[3] A.C. Pigou, 'The Classical Stationary State', *Economic Journal,* Dec 1943.

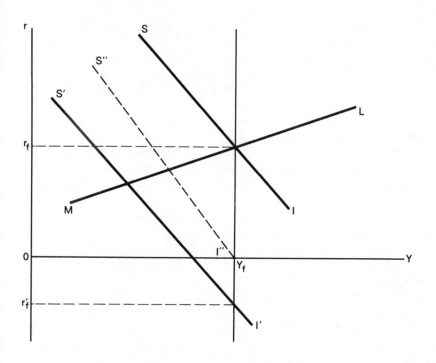

Figure 5.8.2

a change in prices can eliminate the discrepancy by affecting saving. There exists one category of wealth which is affected by a change in the price level, namely the real quantity of money. For a given nominal quantity of money the fall in the price level raises the real quantity of money and therefore the perceived wealth of the community. Thus, if we write the consumption function as

$$C = F\left(Y, \frac{M}{P}\right),$$

a fall in the price level even if it has no effect on the interest rate (the Keynesian case) will still be effective in achieving full employment, not by leading to an increase in investment (via a change in the interest rate), but by increasing consumption (via a change in wealth). In figure 5.8.2, above the change in the price level will shift the *IS* curve to the one marked *I"S"*.

At this stage one could say Keynes is right if the consumption function is of one form; the Classics are right if the consumption function is of another form. That would be a mistake. Pigou's argument is more subtle and more powerful than that.

In the Keynesian case where we have a situation in which people want to save at a zero rate of return, they cannot therefore be saving for the purpose of acquiring future income streams. Why then are they saving? The answer must be that they are saving to acquire wealth for its own sake.[1] They are willing to give up current consumption for the sake of accumulating wealth and therefore must derive some amenity value from the possession of wealth as such. But in that case the consumption function must contain wealth as an argument; the Keynesian case can only arise if wealth is in the consumption function. Thus if wealth is not in the consumption function, the Keynesian case cannot arise; if we have the Keynesian case wealth must be in the consumption function and therefore we also have, via the 'Pigou effect', a solution to the Keynesian problem.

One point should be noted before leaving this discussion. The 'Pigou effect' is based on the idea that changes in the real quantity of money will affect consumption. A change in the real quantity of money can be achieved either by a change in the price level for a given nominal quantity of money, or a change in the nominal quantity of money for a given price level. As far as policy is concerned the 'Pigou effect' is silent about which of these methods of changing the real quantity of money is best. As with all policies the choice has to be made on the basis of all the effects of a given policy. For example, a falling price level might lead to expectations about future changes in the price level which have an undesirable effect. In that case one would achieve the same goal — the change in the real quantity of money — by changing the nominal quantity of money, rather than by relying on the change in the price level.

---

[1] This argument assumes that time preference is not negative, ie, that people are not willing to give up one unit of current consumption to acquire an extra half a unit, say, of future consumption.

references

BAILEY M *National Income and the Price Level* McGraw Hill International 1971.
Chapters 3 and 4.
HICKS J R 'Mr. Keynes and the Classics' in M G Mueller (ed.) *Readings in Macro-economics* Holt, Rinehart and Winston 1966.
KEYNES J M *The General Theory of Employment, Interest and Money* New York 1936.
PATINKIN D 'Price Flexibility and Full Employment' *American Economic Review*
September 1948.
SMITH, Warren L 'A Graphical Exposition of the Complete Keynesian System' in
M G Mueller (ed.) *Readings in Macroeconomics.* Holt, Rinehart and Winston 1966.

chapter 6

the government sector

In most economies government expenditures on goods and services represent a sizable fraction of total expenditures, and via taxation the government also lays claim to a sizable fraction of total income.[1] In this chapter we first examine how the introduction of government expenditures and taxation modifies the model of the economy developed previously (section 6.1). We then examine how the government can use various policies to affect the economic variables in which we are interested — income, employment, the price level and so on — if these are at some 'undesirable' level (sections 6.2, 6.3, 6.4). The analysis of government policies becomes more complicated when we take account of the budget constraint faced by the government (section 6.5), and the effectiveness of policies in achieving their aim more difficult to predict as soon as time lags are introduced into the model (section 6.6). We then go on to briefly examine built-in stabilizers (section 6.7). In the appendix (section 6.8) we examine the effectiveness of fiscal policy given the government budget constraint.

6.1 Real government expenditures and taxation

If it were true that government expenditures on goods and services were determined by the same variables as private sector expenditures, there would be no particular reason why we should treat them separately. For example, if government consumption expenditures were determined by income, and government investment expenditures by the rate of interest (these being the variables we assumed to determine private consumption and investment), we could simply include government expenditures within the categories of consumption and investment which we have analyzed already. However, this does not seem to be the case. We shall therefore assume that government expenditures are policy-determined and not uniquely related to any of the variables in our model.[2]

---

[1] In the UK for example, government expenditures on goods and services are about 30 per cent of Gross National Product.

[2] This of course does not mean that changes in some of the variables in the model will not lead to a change in government policy. A fall in income, for example, may induce the government to undertake some policy to increase income. But there is no automatic connection between the change in income and the change in policy.

The introduction of policy-determined government expenditures poses no difficulties to our analysis of the goods sector. Total desired expenditures now consist of three, rather than two, categories, C, I, and G, where G is the assumed level of government expenditures. The condition for equilibrium in the goods sector now becomes $Y=C+I+G$. The whole analysis carried out in chapters 2 through 6 would remain the same. The only change would be in the specific equation of the IS curve, which shows equilibrium in the goods sector, and would now have to contain an added constant term (G), representing another exogenously determined desired expenditure. However, sad as it may be, government activity is not confined to the acquisition of goods and services for the indulgence of its citizens; the government has, and uses, the power of taxation to acquire claims on resources from the private sector. As taxation reduces the claims to output of the private sector of the economy (its real income) we have to re-examine some of the behavioural assumptions which related desired expenditures to income.[1]

When we discussed consumption (p. 15) we assumed that decisions about how much to consume were made on the basis of individuals' claims to output (their real income). The introduction of taxation reduces the claims to output of the private sector by the amount of taxes collected by the government. Thus the introduction of taxation means that the relevant income variable for private sector decision-making is not total income but disposable income — total income less taxes. Using a linear approximation, the consumption function becomes $C = a+b(Y - T)$ where T represents the taxes collected by the government. In most tax systems T itself is not exogenous but depends on the level of income in the economy; when income changes, the amount of taxes collected by the government changes, and therefore disposable income changes. Let us for simplicity assume a linear approximation for the relationship between taxes and the level of income, say $T=t_0 + tY$, where t_0 is the amount of taxes which is independent of income and t the tax rate which applies to income.[2] Substituting this relationship into the

---

[1] When we discussed the equilibrium condition for the goods sector without a government we saw that we could translate the condition $Y=C+I$ to $S=I$; both meaning that desired expenditures are equal to the claims to output (real income) which in that case equalled total output. We can do a similar translation when a government sector is included. Subdivide the claims to output into two parts, the claims to output of the private sector $(Y - T)$ and the claims to output of the government sector T. The condition that desired expenditures must be equal to total claims to output now becomes

$$(Y - T) + T = C+I+G.$$

$$(6.1.1)$$

Define desired savings as before — the difference between claims to output and desired consumption — thus $S=(Y - T) - C$, substituting this into (6.1.1) we have $S+T = I+G$ which is another way of expressing $Y=C+I+G$.

[2] We defined disposable income as $Y - T$ where T is the amount of taxes collected by the government. If the government also makes transfer payments then T should stand for the *net* taxes collected, ie the difference between total taxes and total transfer payments. Transfer payments, like

consumption function above, we have

$$C = a+b(Y - t_0 - tY)$$

$$= a+b(Y(1 - t) - t_0).$$ \hfill (6.1.2)

Equation (6.1.2) represents the consumption function on the assumption that desired consumption depends on disposable income, and taxes depend on total income.

As far as investment is concerned we shall assume that the introduction of the government sector does not change the relationship we postulated earlier. Substituting the new consumption function (6.1.2) above, and the previous investment function ($I = g_0 - gr$) into the new equilibrium condition for the goods sector, $Y=C+I+G$, we have

$$Y = a+b(Y(1 - t) - t_0)+g_0 - g_r+G$$

$$Y(1 - b(1 - t)) = a - bt_0+g_0 - gr+G$$

$$Y = \frac{1}{1 - b(1 - t)} (a - bt_0+g_0 - gr+G).$$ \hfill (6.1.3)

As we can see equation (6.1.3) is an equation in only two variables, Y and r; the other elements in it are either government-determined constants, t, t_0 and G, or behaviourally determined constants, b, g_0 and g. The equation thus summarizes the equilibrium condition for the goods sector of an economy, which now includes a government, by a relationship between the two variables Y and r. It is essentially no different from equation (2.5.2) in chapter 2 (p. 19) which showed the equilibrium condition for the goods sector for an economy without a government; the multiplier is different, the constant terms are different, but the meaning of the equation, our new *IS* curve, is the same. We recall that the whole analysis of the interrelationships in the economy, in chapters 2 through 5, for which we used the *IS* curve, did not depend on any particular value of the multiplier, or the other parameters of the *IS* curve. We conclude therefore that the introduction of the government sector into our model does not change any of our previous conclusions about the equilibrium conditions for the economy and the

taxes, affect the economy via their effect on disposable income. They should therefore not be confused with government expenditures on goods and services (G). In the tax equation $T=t_0+tY$ we can also include transfer payments. Thus t_0 would now represent the amount of those taxes which are independent of income (eg death duties and other wealth taxes) less the amount of those transfers which are independent of income (eg old age pensions). tY represents the amount of taxes which do depend on income less the amount of transfers which depend on income (eg unemployment insurance and family income supplements).

forces generated in disequilibrium situations. However, we now have three added variables under the control of the government which can be used to affect the equilibrium values of income, employment, the price level, the rate of interest, and so on, when these are not at a level consistent with some policy goal. Before examining the actual mechanics by which this can be done, it may be useful to examine in more general terms the role played by the government in economic activity.

6.2 Government policy

Every government has a number of economic goals which it wants to achieve, and a number of policies that can be used to do this. Sometimes, because of the constraints under which a government must operate, or because of the behavioural relationships that exist in an economy, the government cannot achieve all its goals simultaneously and therefore a problem of choice arises. In this case a decision has to be made as to the 'value' of one goal relative to another. For example, if the constraints facing the government are such that there is a trade off between some level of unemployment and some level of inflation, then even though both full employment and a zero rate of inflation are desirable goals of policy one of these will have to be modified. Even though economic considerations are important in such choices, they are not the only ones that are relevant. What economic analysis can do is to point out the presence of a conflict among goals and the cost of attaining one goal in terms of others. However, these by themselves cannot be enough to dictate a particular course of action, and other information and value judgements are required. An economist may be able to tell that an increase in the growth rate of real national income of y per cent per year might be achieved by diverting x per cent of resources from current consumption to investment, that is to say he may determine the cost of future consumption in terms of current consumption. However, whether it is worthwhile paying this price for increased future consumption is not something that can be decided by the economist; it depends on the value that individuals in the society place on future consumption relative to present consumption. It is especially important to keep these considerations in mind in discussions on government policy, an area in which normative considerations are easily confused with positive ones. Often when one examines disagreements about economic policies one finds that these are not based on disagreements about the economic consequences of the policies, but rather on different tastes for these consequences.

In macroeconomics government policy is usually discussed under two broad headings, fiscal policy and monetary policy. This division is not based on any distinction as to the ultimate goals to be attained but on the basis of the tools used to attain them. We define as fiscal policy any policy in which the government uses its power to tax and make expenditures to attain some given economic goal; as monetary policy any policy in which the government uses its power to change the quantity of money to attain the goal. Besides these two types of policy the government also occasionally uses various types of specific controls to affect the economy. For example, direct control on prices and wages (incomes policy), control of hire purchase terms, control of bank lending, and so on. For the most part we shall not be concerned with any of these except incomes policy.

In chapters 4 and 5 we examined monetary policy when we analyzed the effects of changes in the quantity of money on the equilibrium values of the economic variables in our model. It is true that at the time we had not yet introduced government expenditure and taxation into the goods sector of the model. However, as we saw above, the introduction of government expenditures and taxation only affects the parameters of the *IS* curve, therefore the analysis of the effects of changes in the quantity of money which we carried out earlier needs no modification. So let us turn to fiscal policy.

6.3   Fiscal policy

We saw above that the introduction of the government into the model changes the equation of the *IS* curve to

$$Y = \frac{1}{1 - b(1 - t)} \ (a - bt_0 + g_0 - gr + G)$$

and that fiscal policy involves changing the three government-determined constants t, t_0 and G to attain some economic goal. We therefore want to examine the effects of changes in these on income, employment, the price level and the rate of interest. In figures 6.3.1(a) and (b) the solid lines depict some equilibrium situation in an economy including a government sector, the dashed lines a new equilibrium situation after a change in one of the government variables, say an increase in government expenditures from G^0 to G'.

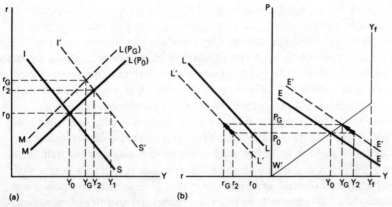

(a)   (b)

Figure 6.3.1

Figure 6.3.1(a) depicts a simple *IS, LM* model of an economy; figure 6.3.1(b) depicts the full model which includes an employment and production sector with an assumed fixed money wage rate of W' (see chapter 5). An increase in government expenditures can be analyzed in the same way as any other exogenous increase in desired expenditures,[1] and can be depicted by a shift in the *IS, EE,* and *LL* curves to $I'S'$, $E'E'$ and $L'L'$ respectively. We know from our previous analysis that the *IS* curve shifts by the change in expenditures times the multiplier. Thus if ΔG represents the change in government expenditures (from G^0 to G') then the *IS* curve shifts by (see figure 6.3.1)

$$Y_1 - Y_0 = \Delta Y = \Delta G \, \frac{1}{1 - b\,(1 - t)}. \qquad (6.3.1)$$

Of course by now we know that even in the simple *IS, LM* model the change in income will not be $Y_1 - Y_0$ unless the *LM* curve is perfectly elastic. If it is not, then the increase in government expenditures will lead to a rise in the rate of interest from r_0 to r_2 which will reduce another element of desired expenditure, namely investment. Thus the actual change in income, ignoring the production and employment sector, will be less than the shift in the *IS* curve. In figure 6.3.1(a) income rises from Y_0 to Y_2. The change in income from Y_0 to Y_2 is also shown in figure 6.3.1(b) as the rightward shift in the *EE* curve to $E'E'$ and the change in the interest rate from r_0 to r_2 is shown as the leftward shift in the *LL* curve to $L'L'$. If the price level remained at P_0 this would be the end of the story. We know, however, that the increase in aggregate demand in our model leads to a rise in prices, in our case from P_0 to P_G (shown by the arrows along the $E'E'$ and $L'L'$ curves). This rise in prices reduces the real quantity of money in the economy (the shift in the *LM* curve from *LM* (P_0) to *LM* (P_G)), raises the interest rate even further to r_G, and therefore reduces desired investment.[2] The actual change in income arising from the initial change in government expenditures is thus from Y_0 to the new equilibrium level Y_G, shown in both figures 6.3.1(a) and (b). The story told above could have been much shortened, and the denouement reached directly, by just looking at figure 6.3.1(b) where the final equilibrium values of all the variables, Y_G, r_G and P_G, can be read off directly after the two curves have been shifted in the appropriate direction, but such a summary would cover up much of the underlying economics.

We can now move on quickly to examine the effects of a change in taxation. We can

---

[1] By an exogenous change in desired expenditures we mean here (as usual) any change *not* caused by a change in any of the endogenous variables in the model; in our case Y, r and P.

[2] It should be stressed again that the shift in the *LM* curve does not occur because of any change in monetary policy. The nominal quantity of money has not changed. Thus the $E'E'$ and $L'L'$ curves do *not* shift again. The change in the *LM* curve due to a change in the price level is already incorporated in the *EE* and *LL* curves. The movement of the price level *along* the $E'E'$ and $L'L'$ curves is represented by a shift in the *LM* curve to *LM* (P_G).

still use figures 6.3.1(a) and (b) for this but we must now assume that the initial change in the *IS* curve occurred because of a cut in the fixed tax from t_0 to t', rather than an increase in expenditures from G_0 to G'. The shift in the *IS* curve in this case is equal to

$$Y_1 - Y_0 = \Delta Y = -b\Delta t_0 \cdot \frac{1}{1 - b(1 - t)}. \tag{6.3.2}$$

Except for this difference in the initial shift of the *IS* curve, everything else is the same as in the analysis of the change in government expenditures carried out above.

It is useful to see why in equation (6.3.2) the multiplier is applied to the expression $-b\Delta t_0$ *not* to the change in taxes which is equal to Δt_0. We recall that the multiplier shows how a change in desired expenditures affects the equilibrium condition in the goods sector of the economy, ie it measures the shift of the *IS* curve arising from a change in desired expenditures. What element of desired expenditures changes is totally irrelevant to the size of the multiplier, only the size of the change is relevant. A change in taxes is by itself not a change in desired expenditures. It is only via the behavioural assumption that desired consumption is a function of disposable income, and the relationship between disposable income and taxes, that a change in taxes leads to a change in desired expenditures. These are the relationships described by equation (6.1.2) (p. 90). From that equation we can see that a change in taxes of Δt_0 changes desired consumption by $-b\Delta t_0$. It is to this change in desired expenditure that we should apply the multiplier, to get a shift in the *IS* curve of $-b\Delta t_0 \left[\frac{1}{1 - b(1 - t)} \right]$.[1]

In the case of a change in government expenditures, ΔG does measure the change in desired expenditures and thus the multiplier is applied to it directly. We can see from the above discussion that the effect of a change in taxes on income depends critically on the relationship that we postulate between taxes and desired consumption (or of course any other element of desired expenditures). This consideration will be important later when we discuss different theories of the consumption function.

---

[1] Using these ideas we can easily see the initial shift in the *IS* curve if t (the tax rate which applies to income) changes by Δt. Rewrite equation (6.1.2) as

$C = a + bY - bY t - bt_0$

$\therefore \Delta C = -bY\Delta t.$

This shows the initial change in consumption due to the change in the tax rate. Applying the multiplier to this change in desired expenditures, we get

$$\Delta Y = -bY\Delta t \cdot \frac{1}{1 - b(1 - t)}.$$

6.4   Incomes policy

As mentioned earlier, besides monetary and fiscal policies governments have attempted
to use various types of specific controls to affect the economy. One of these has been
incomes policy, which is an attempt to control wages and prices. Even though the aim
of incomes policy is usually formulated in terms of controlling the rate at which money
wages and prices are allowed to change rather than in terms of a once and for all change
in these, we can get some insight into this policy by looking at the effects of imposed
changes in the level of money wages and prices within the framework of our static
model of the economy. In figure 6.4.1 the solid lines represent some equilibrium of the
economy with a given money wage rate of W_o, with equilibrium income and price levels
of Y_o and P_o respectively. Assume now that the government by statutory control lowers
the money wage rate to W' (but makes no attempt to control prices). The new aggregate
supply curve is now the dashed line $W'Y_F$. The new equilibrium occurs with an income
level of Y', and a price level of P'. Even though only money wages are controlled, prices
are also affected. This is not surprising. At the initial price level P_o and the controlled
money wage W' there is an excess of aggregate supply. Real wages are lower than before
and therefore employment and output greater. It is this excess of aggregate supply
which leads to the fall in prices to P', even though no controls have been imposed on
prices. However, the fall in prices from P_o to P' is less than the fall in money wages
from W_o to W'. Thus real wages have fallen, although not by the full amount of the fall
in money wages. It is exactly because real wages have fallen that output has increased
from Y_o to Y'.

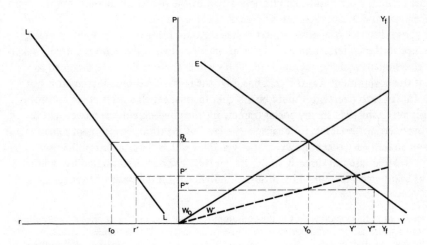

Figure 6.4.1

Assume, however, that the government also attempts to control and reduce prices by the same proportion as the cut in wages, ie reduce prices to P''. In this case real wages remain the same and employment and output remain the same. However, at the price level P'' there is an excess of aggregate demand of $Y''-Y_0$. The fall in prices has increased aggregate demand from Y_0 to Y'' but given that the real wage rate has not fallen the quantity of output supplied has remained the same. This excess of aggregate demand would make it very difficult to maintain the price level at P'' and therefore the prices aspect of the incomes policy, unless the incomes policy were accompanied by some other policy to cut down aggregate demand. We can also see from the figure that if only prices are controlled, say at P'', while the money wage rate remains at W_0 we also have an excess of aggregate demand over output. Output actually falls, because of the rise in real wages induced by the fall in prices.

Within the framework of our model we can analyze many other types of specific government controls by first examining their effect on one or another of the behavioural functions that enter into the model. Take for example control over hire-purchase terms. This policy attempts to reduce the purchases of consumer durables which are an element in the consumption function. Thus if the policy is successful it will lead to a shift of the consumption function.[1] The effect of this policy on the various economic variables can then be traced out as above by using the *IS, EE* and other relevant curves. Of course to know what the magnitude of the effect will be we would have to know what is the magnitude of the effect of changing hire-purchase terms on desired consumption. Similarly, control over bank advances is an attempt to affect consumption or investment or both, ie if successful leads to a shift in the consumption function or the investment function or both. The ultimate effect of the policy on income, employment, the price level, and so on, can then be traced out in our model.

The above discussion of government policies should bring out one point of great importance to the understanding of the relationship between the actions actually taken by the government and the economic variables which these actions are designed to affect. If the government wants to change, say, the level of national income it is not very useful for it to decree 'let there be a higher income'; such a method of control is no longer very effective. In any social framework the government has power, within limits, over certain variables; for example the level of taxation, government expenditures, and so on. Very often, however, the variables which government policy is designed to affect are not directly under its control. They are determined by the interaction of many decisions taken by different individuals on the basis of their goals, and

[1] Formally what this means is that in the consumption function $a+b(Y(1-t) - t_0)$, a incorporates all the factors which affect consumption except disposable income. If hire-purchase terms are relevant to consumption decisions they are included in a and changes in a represent shifts of the consumption function.

the economic constraints as they see them. In order to affect these variables the government has to manipulate the decisions taken by these individuals by changing the constraints facing them. How effective the government will be in this manipulation will depend on the importance of the variables the government does control, to the decisions made by individuals. If the relevant constraint variable in the consumption decision is disposable income, then by its control over taxation the government can affect consumption, and via this the level of income. The weaker is the relationship between consumption decisions and disposable income the more irrelevant is the power over taxation to the control of income. To understand what control a government has over an economy it is therefore not enough to know what variables the government actually controls, one has to know besides how these variables are related to the decisions of individuals.

6.5   The government budget constraint

One of the problems in analyzing the effects of government policy is the interrelationship among the various policies. When analyzing monetary policy we examine the effects of changes in the quantity of money while holding government expenditures and taxes constant. This is done implicitly when we shift the *LM* curve along a *given IS* curve, thus assuming that it is possible to change the quantity of money without changing expenditures or taxation.[1] Similarly in this chapter we examined the effects of changes in taxation, holding government expenditures and the quantity of money constant; and the effects of changes in government expenditures, holding the level of taxation and the quantity of money constant. We showed fiscal policy as a shift in the *IS* curve along a given *LM* curve. What the above implies is that it is sensible to consider the effect of changing government expenditures (or taxes, or the quantity of money) while holding the other government policy variables constant. Let us examine this question in more detail.

Assume for a moment that a government can finance its expenditures only by collecting taxes (T) or by printing currency (C_u) and start from an initial situation in which the budget is balanced, government expenditures being equal to tax receipts $(G=T)$. Then it must be true that

$$\Delta G = \Delta T + \Delta C_u. \tag{6.5.1}$$

Equation (6.5.1) states that the government can change its expenditure only by changing taxes by the same amount, or by changing the quantity of currency in the economy by that amount, or by some combination of the two. In this case it is contradictory to

---

[1] We did this in chapters 4 (p. 52) and 5 (p. 74) before we had explicitly introduced government expenditures and taxation into the model. But we argued above (p. 92) that the introduction of government does not change the analysis of monetary policy.

consider the effect of a change in government expenditures holding taxes *and* the quantity of money constant. Given the budget constraint of the government, defined by equation (6.5.1) this is not possible. Similarly with the other two policy variables ΔT and ΔC_u. If we change one, then we either have to change the other or change G.

We can still examine, say, the effect of a change in government expenditures, but to get an answer we have to know how these expenditures were financed; the results will be quite different depending on the financing used. In figure 6.5.1 assume that we start from an initial equilibrium situation at Y_e and r_e respectively. Assume now that the government increases its expenditures by ΔG shown by the shift of *IS* to *I'S'* which is equal to

$$\Delta G \; \frac{1}{1 - b \, (1 - t)}.$$

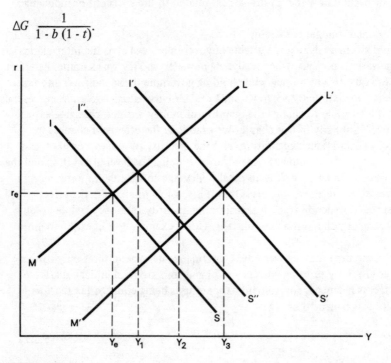

Figure 6.5.1

If we stop there we would find that the change in income induced by the change in G is from Y_e to Y_2.[1] However, as the previous discussion has shown, we cannot stop there. If the expenditures were financed by an increase in taxes, shown by a shift of

[1] We are here looking at only the initial effect and ignoring the production and employment sector.

the *IS* curve to $I''S''$, which is equal to $\Delta G. \dfrac{1-b}{1-b(1-t)}$, then the change in income induced by the government expenditure policy is $Y_1 - Y_e$.[1] If, however, the expenditures were financed by changing the money supply, income changes to Y_3, which is a combination of the simple expenditure change with a change in monetary policy, shown by the shift in the *LM* curve to $L'M'$. Start now with the equilibrium situation represented by Y_3 and assume the government wants to reduce the quantity of money by an amount that will shift the $L'M'$ curve back to the *LM* curve. What will the effect of this be on the level of income? Again the answer depends on how the quantity of money is reduced. From the budget constraint above we know that there are two ways in which this can be done. The government can maintain its expenditures but increase taxes, or it can maintain taxes but decrease expenditures. Both actions will result in a budget surplus and the money so collected and held by the government is the fall in the money supply which shifted the $L'M'$ curve to the *LM* curve. Thus the final level of income will be Y_0 if expenditures are cut, Y_1 if taxes are increased.

If we allow for the possibility of government borrowing, and take into account the effects of changes in the quantity of currency on the supply of money, the financing constraint of the government is more complicated than the one shown by equation (6.5.1) above. The government can now finance its expenditures either by taxes, or by printing money, or by issuing bonds — borrowing from the private sector. Again starting from an initial situation of a balanced budget ($G=T$) we have,[2]

$$\Delta G = \Delta T + \Delta C_u + \Delta B_g, \qquad\qquad (6.5.2)$$

where B_g is the change in government bonds outstanding. However, we know from our analysis of the supply of money that, in a partial reserve system, if currency outstanding changes by C_u the quantity of money supplied changes by $h\,C_u$ where h is the money

---

[1] The shift from *IS* to $I'S'$ is equal to $\Delta G. \dfrac{1}{1-b(1-t)}$. The shift from $I'S'$ to $I''S''$ is equal to $-b\,\Delta t_0. \dfrac{1}{1-b(1-t)}$ (see p. 94). However, by assumption $\Delta G = \Delta t_0$ therefore the shift from *IS* to $I''S''$ is equal to

$$\Delta G \left[\dfrac{1}{1-b(1-t)} - \dfrac{b}{1-b(1-t)}\right]$$

$$= \Delta G. \dfrac{1-b}{1-b(1-t)}.$$

[2] We start from an initial balanced budget situation to keep the technical analysis less complicated. If the initial situation were one in which, say, $G > T$, then in the initial situation C or B_g was changing, therefore a further change in G would affect the *rate* of change of one of these variables.

multiplier (see chapter 3, p. 37), therefore

$$\Delta C_u = \frac{\Delta M^s}{h}.$$

Substituting this into (6.5.2) above,

$$\Delta G = \Delta T + \frac{\Delta M^s}{h} + \Delta B_g. \tag{6.5.3}$$

As with equation (6.5.1) above, equation (6.5.3) defines the fixed relationship between the government-controlled variables (G, T, M^s, B_g) on the assumption that h is given.[1] Any one of these can be changed holding two of the others constant, but not holding the other three constant. Now we can vary, say, government expenditures holding taxes and the money supply constant, but only by varying the quantity of government bonds outstanding in the same direction. Similarly with the other variables. Thus with the budget constraint shown in equation (6.5.3) it is no longer contradictory to examine the effects of changing one government policy alone, *as long as* we remember that the offsetting change necessitated by the budget constraint occurs in the quantity of government bonds outstanding. We can do this only because the quantity of government bonds does not enter into any of the behavioural functions in our model, therefore changes in the quantity do not affect the equilibrium values of any of the variables in the model.[2]

---

[1] If h is also considered as a policy parameter (because it depends on the reserve requirement) we have

$$M^s = hC_u$$

$$\Delta M^s = C_u \Delta h + h \Delta C_u$$

$$\Delta C_u = \frac{\Delta M^s}{h} - C_u \frac{\Delta h}{h} \text{ but, } C_u = \frac{M^s}{h}$$

hence $\Delta C_u = \frac{\Delta M^s}{h} - M^s \frac{\Delta h}{h^2}$

substituting this into equation (6.5.2) above the government constraint becomes

$$\Delta G = \Delta T + \frac{\Delta M^s}{h} - M^s \frac{\Delta h}{h^2} + \Delta B_g.$$

[2] This problem is discussed in more detail in the appendix.

6.6   Time lags

The analysis of government policy presented above may give the impression that if the government has control over taxation, expenditures and the money supply, it should have perfect or near-perfect control over income, employment, the price level, and so on. This impression will be quickly dispelled when we examine, albeit very briefly, one of the most difficult problems connected with the control of economic activity: the problem of timing. In the model of the economy presented above, time was not a relevant variable. When we examined how changes in one variable affect another, we did not ask whether the change would start affecting the other variable right away, or how long it would take before the full effect would work itself out. We were doing comparative statics, comparing an initial equilibrium situation with a new equilibrium situation, rather than dynamics, examining the path by which the economy moves from one equilibrium situation to another, and the time pattern of this path. An analysis of economic dynamics is outside the scope of this book, but we can indicate the problems posed by time by looking at the problem posed to economic control by the existence of time lags.

By a lag we simply mean that there is a time span between the occurrence of some event and the effect produced by that event. The reasons for the existence of the lag are not important for our purposes. It could be that the behavioural relationship connecting the two events is such that time is required for the cause to be transmitted into an effect; it could be that because of lack of knowledge the occurrence of the first event is not known for some time; or it could be that because of some institutional constraints it takes time to implement certain actions. In figure 6.6.1 below we measure

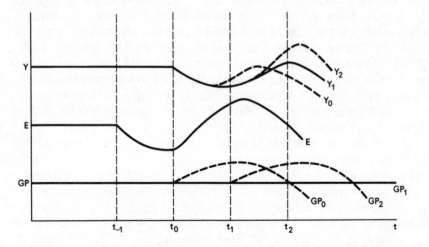

Figure 6.6.1

time on the horizontal axis. On the vertical axis Y represents income, E represents some economic variable that has an effect on income, for example investment, the balance of trade, the demand for money and so on; GP represents some government policy variable which also has an effect on income, for example government expenditures, taxation, or the supply of money. We shall use the convention of measuring changes in E and GP by the direction of the effect that these changes have on the level of income. Thus if E represents investment, a rise in E represents an increase in investment; if E represents the demand for money a rise in E represents a fall in the demand for money (because a fall in the demand for money, for a given supply, leads to a fall in the interest rate and via this to a rise in income). Similarly, if GP represents government expenditures, a rise in GP represents an increase in expenditures; if GP represents taxation a rise in GP represents a fall in taxes.

In figure 6.6.1 we represent a situation in which the level of all the variables is constant up to period t_{-1}. At time t_{-1} E starts falling and moves over time as shown by the solid curve. The solid line marked Y_1 shows how the movement of E affects the level of income on the assumption that the government policy variable remains constant at the level marked GP_1. We have constructed a situation in which there is a lag in the effect of E on Y. E starts falling in period t_{-1}, but Y does not start falling until period t_0. Assume now that the government starts using its policy as soon as it observes that income starts falling, ie in period t_0, and that government policy follows the path shown by the dashed line GP_0. The dashed line marked Y_0 shows the path of income over time with this government policy. Income continues to fall unabated until period t_1, at which point the government policy introduced in periods t_0 starts working and the fall in income is checked. We have assumed that there is a one-period lag between an initial change in policy and the effect of this on income. Now assume that the government policy is not introduced until period t_1, and changes as shown by the dashed line GP_2. This lag in the introduction of the policy may arise because it is not realized that income has fallen until after the event (this is called a recognition lag), or because it takes time to introduce a policy (this is called an implementation lag). Now the dashed line marked Y_2 shows the movement of income over time with this particular path of the government variable. In this case the government policy leads to an increase in the fluctuation of income.

The highly stylized representation of figure 6.6.1 brings out most of the problems that arise in the attempt to control economic activity. First, there is the problem of recognizing when a policy becomes necessary. In our example the events which lead to the fall in income occur in period t_{-1}; at this time income remained unchanged. If one could predict not only that these events will lead to a fall in income, but also when this fall will occur, one could start implementing the government policy at some point between t_{-1} and t_0 so that the policy will start having an effect at t_0 and stop the fall in income. Second, there is the problem raised by the lag between the implementation of the policy and the effect of the policy on Y. In our example the policy implemented at t_0 does not have an effect on income until t_1. In the example the policy is still partially effective in reducing the degree of fluctuation in Y. However, what if the lag were greater? The policy would then start affecting income in period t_2, say, and the effect of this may be to change the time path of income to that shown by Y_2, thus leading to a greater degree of fluctuation in income than that which occurs without any change in policy.

6.7   Built-in stabilizers
One way of avoiding some of the problems raised by the existence of the various lags is to structure some of the government policy variables in such a way that they will react automatically to any change which has to be offset. We have already come across one such policy variable, namely taxation. When taxes are a function of income, any change in income changes the amount of taxes collected by the government in the same direction without any specific change of government policy. Assume that GP in figure 6.6.1 represents government taxation. If taxes are independent of income then the solid line marked GP_1 would represent the movement of taxes over time as income moves in the way shown by the solid line Y_1. If, however, taxes depended on income then the line marked GP_0 might represent the movement of taxes over time (remembering the measuring convention we are using) and the level of income might be shown by the line marked Y_0. If the lag in introducing a government policy was a recognition or an implementation lag as with GP_2, then the automatic response of taxes to income overcomes this problem; taxes change automatically as soon as income starts changing. If, however, the lag is of the type represented by GP_0 (which represents a lag in the effect of the policy on income) then what is needed is some change in a policy variable which is tied directly to the change in E (that will occur at t_{-1}) rather than to Y.

The above discussion of taxes as automatic stabilizers can be easily extended to all sorts of transfers which are income-related either directly or indirectly, for example, unemployment benefits and family income supplements (see note 1. p. 89).

6.8   Appendix
We saw in this chapter how the government budget constraint imposes certain limitations on government policy. Any fiscal or monetary policy results in a change in at least two of the variables in the budget constraint. This fact, combined with a more rigorous analysis of the demand for money, raises some important issues about the effectiveness of fiscal policy in changing the level of income. Some of these issues are at the heart of the current debate about 'monetarism' — the idea that monetary policy is effective and important.

The discussion of the speculative motive of the demand for money in chapter 3 section 3.2 was based on a theory of portfolio allocation among risky and non-risky assets. An individual's taste for risk and the interest rate determines what fraction of his portfolio he holds in the form of non-risky assets, namely money, and what fraction in the form of income yielding risky assets, namely bonds. However, the demand for money (and, of course, bonds) also depends on the total size of the portfolio to be allocated among the assets. For a given taste for risk, and a given interest rate, the total size of the portfolio is larger, the larger is the demand for both money and bonds. Assume now that the government issues £100 of bonds. What effect will this have on the demand for money and the interest rate?

From the government budget constraint we know that the increase in government bonds outstanding can occur in one of three ways; a cut in taxes for given expenditures, an increase in expenditures for given taxes, or a decrease in the quantity of money. If the increase in bonds occurred via a cut in taxes, or an increase in government expenditures, the total size of the portfolio of wealth to be allocated among money and bonds increases by the full £100 increase in government bonds. For a given taste for risk and a given interest rate, the demand for money therefore increases (there is a shift in the demand curve for money to the right). For a given supply curve of money the interest rate will rise. If the increase in government bonds occurred via a decrease in the quantity of money, nothing happens to the size of the portfolio. We have a straightforward change in the supply of money, ie a movement along a given demand curve for money.

In figure 6.8.1 we incorporate the above analysis of the demand for money with the government budget constraint, to examine the effects of fiscal policy. Assume we start from some initial situation at time t_0, in an equilibrium represented by the curves marked *IS* and *LM* (t_0), with income Y_0 and the interest rate r_0. Now the government increases expenditures for given taxes, or cuts taxes for given expenditures. This is shown by the shift of the *IS* curve $I'S'$. From the government budget constraint we know that to achieve this policy the government has to finance the resulting budget deficit either by increasing the quantity of money or the quantity of bonds. Assume that the deficit is financed by an increase in the quantity of bonds. From the previous analysis of the demand for money we know that the increase in the quantity of government bonds will lead to an increase in the demand for money, which can, for example, be represented by a shift of the *LM* curve to the one marked *LM* (t_1). The new equilibrium level of income, Y_1, could be higher or lower than the old. In our example we have assumed that it is higher. We cannot, however, stop here.

If the *IS* curve stays at $I'S'$, ie if the government maintains its new level of expenditures or taxes, the deficit continues and the government has to continue increasing the quantity of bonds outstanding. Thus in the next period the *LM* curve shifts again to *LM* (t_2), say, even though nothing has happened to the *IS* curve. The *LM* curve will continue shifting as long as the *IS* curve stays at $I'S'$. The *LM* curve will only stop shifting when the quantity of bonds stops increasing. This will occur if the government

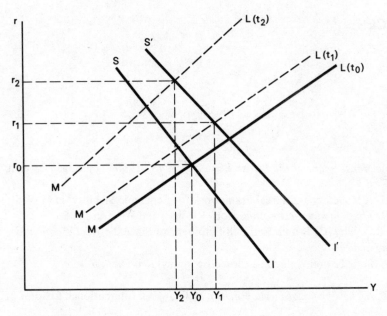

Figure 6.8.1

reverses its fiscal policy and the *IS* curve shifts back to its original level.[1]

In the above example the government policy which effectively increased income in period one (when it was introduced) ultimately leads to a fall in income, to Y_2, in the next period, and of course to further falls in income in future periods.

[1] A similar analysis applies to a deficit financed by the creation of money rather than bonds.

references

DOW J C R *The Management of the British Economy 1945 - 1960* Cambridge University Press 1971.

FRIEDMAN M 'A Monetary and Fiscal Framework for Economic Stability' in M G Mueller (ed.) *Readings in Macroeconomics* Holt, Rinehart and Winston 1966.

MATHEWS R C O 'Why has Britain Had Full Employment Since the War?' *Economic Journal* September 1968.

PHILLIPS A W 'Stabilisation Policy in a Closed Economy' *Economic Journal* January 1954.

MUSGRAVE R A *The Theory of Public Finance* McGraw Hill International. Chapter 21.

chapter 7

the international sector

The basic element introduced by international trade is that countries can use goods which they themselves do not produce, they can 'get' goods from other countries – imports; and they can dispose of goods which they themselves do not want to use, they can 'give' goods to other countries – exports. The constraints facing individuals in an open economy can thus be different from those they face in a closed one. Of course 'getting' goods from other countries and 'giving' goods to other countries is seldom an act of charity. If it involves an exchange of goods for goods, the constraint facing individuals in an open economy as far as the use of goods is concerned is still total output. If, however, it involves an exchange of goods for some form of wealth, it means that individuals in an open economy can use more or less goods than they produce by reducing or increasing their claims to future goods. It is the possibility of the latter type of exchange which forces us to re-examine the condition for equilibrium in the goods sector, once we allow for international trade (section 7.1). International trade and international capital transactions involve currency flows among countries, so we examine the balance of payments (section 7.2) and the effect of domestic variables on the balance of payments (section 7.3). This leads to an examination of the conditions for internal and external equilibrium (section 7.4). We then look at various policies to achieve balance of payments equilibrium and their effects on the domestic economy (sections 7.5, 7.6, 7.7.)

7.1 Trade and the goods sector

The condition for equilibrium in the goods sector of a closed economy was defined as a situation in which people demand all the goods available to the economy. In a closed economy the quantity of goods available is equal to the output of the economy (Y); in an open economy we must add to this the goods available from other economies, ie imports (M). In a closed economy we subdivided the uses of goods into three categories (C, I, and G), in an open economy we must add another category, 'giving' goods to other economies, ie exports (X). The equilibrium condition in the goods sector of an open economy is therefore $Y+M=C+I+G+X$. Rearranging terms we have

$Y+M=C+I+G+X$. Rearranging terms we have $Y=C+I+G+(X-M)$.
$Y=C+I+G+(X-M)$.

$$(7.1.1)$$

The first three terms on the right-hand side of equation (7.1.1) represent the desired expenditures by residents of the economy; what they want to consume, invest, and use in the form of government expenditures, call this total (*D*). The expression in the brackets in equation (7.1.1) is the difference between exports and imports, which represents the real balance of trade; call this (*B*). Thus the equilibrium condition for an open economy becomes

$$Y = D + B. \tag{7.1.2}$$

Equation (7.1.2) brings out the points mentioned in the first paragraph. If *B=O*, exports are equal to imports. People are receiving goods from other countries by giving up an equal amount of goods produced at home; we have an exchange of goods for goods. In this case in equilibrium *Y=D;* desired expenditures of residents are equal to the output of the domestic economy, and people are using up only the amount of goods they are producing. If *B* is greater than zero, exports are greater than imports, in equilibrium *D* is less than *Y;* residents are using up less goods than they are producing and are therefore either giving them away or are acquiring some form of wealth in return. If *B* is less than zero, imports are greater than exports so that in equilibrium *D* is greater than *Y;* residents are using up more goods than they are producing and are therefore either receiving them free, or are giving up some form of wealth for them.

The equilibrium condition expressed in equations (7.1.1) and (7.1.2) above contains two new variables, *M* and *X*. To be able to incorporate these into our model of the economy we have to make some behavioural assumptions about their determinants, just as we did previously about the determinants of the other variables in the model. As far as imports are concerned we shall assume that they are positively related to the disposable real income in the economy, and positively related to the price level in the economy *relative* to the price level in the rest of the world. We assumed previously that consumption in general was a function of disposable income, and as disposable income rises people want to consume more of all goods. If imports are not inferior then they will also want to consume more of these goods. The reason for including the relative price level of the domestic economy and the rest of the world as a determinant of imports is that we assume that imports and domestically produced goods are substitutes, so that when domestic prices rise relative to world prices people will substitute foreign goods for domestic goods, so that imports will rise. As far as exports are concerned we shall assume that they depend on the domestic price level relative to that of the rest of the world. The reason for this assumption is identical to that given above for imports. As the domestic price level rises relative to that of the rest of the world, foreigners will tend to buy more of their own domestically produced goods which have become relatively cheaper and thus import less, which means that the exports of the domestic economy will fall.[1]

If, for simplicity, we express the above behavioural assumptions in linear form, we have

$$M = m_o + m_1 Y_D + m_2 \frac{eP}{P_w} \tag{7.1.3}$$

$$\text{and } X = x_o - x_1 \frac{eP}{P_w} \tag{7.1.4}$$

where m_o and x_o represent the component of imports and exports which are independent of either disposable income or relative prices, Y_D is domestic disposable income, P the domestic price level, P_w the world price level, and e the exchange rate.[2] The signs in the equations follow the previous discussion where it was argued that imports are positively related to both domestic disposable income and relative prices, and exports are negatively related to relative prices. The real balance of trade (B) was defined as $X - M$, hence

$$B = x_o - m_o - m_1 \, Y_D - (x_1 + m_2) \frac{eP}{P_w}.$$

Let $x_o - m_o = B_o$ and $x_1 + m_2 = B_1$ then

$$B = B_o - m_1 Y_D - B_1 \frac{eP}{P_w}. \tag{7.1.5}$$

Using the simple tax relationship assumed in the last chapter, $T = t_o + tY$, we have $Y_D = Y - T = Y(1 - t) - t_o$, hence

$$B = B_o - m_1 \, (Y(1 - t) - t_o) - B_1 \frac{eP}{P_w}. \tag{7.1.6}$$

Equation (7.1.6) represents our assumptions about the determinants of the balance of

---

[1] As with imports above we would expect that exports also depend on the level of real income in the rest of the world. For simplicity we shall assume throughout this chapter that this does not change.

[2] The exchange rate must be included to convert the prices to comparable units. If the price of a good is £5 in the UK and $4 in the US, their relative price is 5/4 *only* if the exchange rate is 1. If the exchange rate is, say, 2, ie the price of one pound is $2, then the relative price of the goods is $\frac{eP}{P_w} = 5/2$.

trade. The balance of trade is negatively related to disposable income because imports are positively related to disposable income; and negatively related to the relative price level because a rise in this both reduces exports and increases imports, and both of these are adverse to the balance of trade.

If we make the same assumptions about the determinants of domestic expenditures as we made previously, we have $D=C+I+G = a+b(Y(1 - t) - t_o) + g_o - gr + G$ (see equation (6.1.3) p. 98). Substituting equation (7.1.6) and the above expression for D into the equilibrium condition for the goods sector in an open economy, $Y=D+B$, we get

$$Y= a+ b \left(Y(1 - t) - t_o\right) + g_o - gr + G+ B_o - m_1 \left(Y(1 - t) - t_o\right) - B_1 \frac{eP}{P_w}$$

simplifying and rearranging terms,

$$Y = \frac{1}{1 - (b - m_1)(1 - t)} \left[a - t_o (b - m_1) + g_o - gr+G+B_o - B_1 \frac{eP}{P_w}\right]. \tag{7.1.7}$$

Equation (7.1.7) shows the equilibrium condition for the goods sector of an open economy incorporating all the behavioural assumptions we made. The equation thus represents the *IS* curve for an open economy. For given values of the exchange rate (e) and the world price level (P_w) equilibrium in the goods sector of an open economy depends on real income, the interest rate *and* the domestic price level. The only difference between this *IS* curve and the versions of the *IS* curve we used before is that it is an equation in three domestic variables, Y, r and P rather than only the first two. This makes diagrammatic representation more complicated, but conceptually it is no more difficult than the others.

Figure 7.1.1(a) shows three different *IS* curves for three different price levels where $P_2 > P_1 > P_0$. We assume throughout that the world price level and the exchange rate are at some given level and do not change.[1] In the figure we also show the three *LM* curves for the three price levels. Points *A*, *B*, and *C* represent the three equilibrium situations in the goods and money sectors for the three different price levels. In figure 7.1.1(b) we incorporate the goods and money sectors with an employment and output sector incorporating a fixed money wage rate of W_o, in the same way as we did in chapter 5. As far as the shape of the *EE* curve is concerned, the fact that the *IS* curve, incorporating the trade sector is now a function of the price level does not matter. The *EE* curve is still downward-sloping, showing a negative relationship between real income and the price level. However, the introduction of the trade sector might affect the slope of the *LL* curve. As can be seen from figure 7.1.1(a) the relationship between the

[1] A change in either of these would shift all the *IS* curves in figure 7.1.1(a).

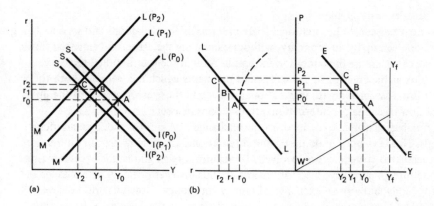

Figure 7.1.1

price level and the rate of interest can be positive or negative depending on whether changes in the price level shift the *IS* curve by more or less than the *LM* curve. Thus the *LL* curve could look like the dashed line in figure 7.1.1(b) rather than the solid line. We shall continue to assume that it looks like the solid line, ie that the magnitudes of the behavioural parameters in the two sectors are such that changes in the price level shift the *LM* curve by more than the *IS* curve. It should be noted that this is an empirical assumption rather than something arising from the general behavioural assumptions we have made so far.

One point should be noted before leaving figure 7.1.1. Both the *EE* and *LL* curves are derived for given conditions of aggregate demand, ie given *IS* and *LM* curves. These are the things that are held constant along these two curves. With the introduction of international trade, and our assumption that trade depends on the relative price level of the domestic economy and the rest of the world, the world price level and the exchange rate will affect aggregate demand via their effect on the real balance of trade (*B*). Thus the world price level and the exchange rate are also held constant along the *EE* and *LL* curves.[1] If, for example, the world price level rises, exports will rise, imports will fall and the balance of trade will increase. This will shift the *EE* curve to the right and the *LL* curve to the left, just as any other increase in aggregate demand; hence it will increase the domestic price level, interest rate, and real income if the last was at a less than full employment level before the change.

[1] It is a useful exercise to work out the effect of changes in the exchange rate and the world price level on the *LL* and *EE* curves via their effects on the *IS* curve. See note (p. 110).

7.2   The balance of payments

So far we have discussed international trade in terms of the real goods and services being acquired or given up by an economy, without examining the associated financial flows. Before we can examine the condition for equilibrium in the international sector we have to look at the concept of the balance of payments which incorporates both the financial flows associated with international trade, and those associated with the international flow of capital, ie international transactions in assets.

In a non-barter world, trade involves the exchange of goods for money, and money for goods. This is so both in domestic and international trade. However, in international trade at least two currencies are involved. To acquire foreign goods it is necessary first to acquire foreign currency. International trade thus involves not only an exchange of goods for goods, but also an exchange of money for money. Money is not, however, a free good and has a price like all other goods. This price is called the exchange rate and measures the price of domestic currency in terms of foreign currency. For example, at the time of writing, the price of £1 in terms of dollars is around $2.40. Given the exchange rate, we can convert the real balance of trade previously discussed into the financial flows that it generates in terms of foreign currency. If X represents some real quantity of exports and P the domestic price of exports then PX represents the value of exports in terms of domestic currency. If e represents the exchange rate, then ePX measures the inflow of foreign currency generated by this amount of exports. If M is the quantity of imports and P_w the foreign price of imports then P_wM represents the value of imports measured in terms of foreign currency,[1] and therefore the outflow of foreign currency generated by imports. The net flow of foreign currency generated by international trade is thus

$$ePX - P_wM. \tag{7.2.1}$$

International capital flows occur when residents of one country acquire assets belonging to residents of another. For example, if a British resident buys a US bond he is exchanging domestic currency for an income stream denominated in US currency and there is a capital flow *out* of the UK. If an American company buys up a UK firm, it is exchanging US currency for an expected income stream denominated in UK currency and there is a capital flow *into* the UK.[2] Just as with international trade, international asset transactions require first an exchange of money for money. To acquire a US asset the British resident must first acquire US currency, and the same thing applies to the US firm acquiring the UK firm. Let K represent the *net* inflow of

---

[1] The value of imports measured in terms of domestic currency is $\dfrac{P_w}{e}M$.

[2] It should be noted that the direction of the capital flow is defined by the direction of the currency flow, not the direction of the flow of assets.

foreign currency generated by international capital transactions, which of course may be positive or negative. The balance of payments is defined as the total of all currency flows generated by both international trade and international asset transactions. Using the previous notations and letting *BP* stand for the balance of payments in terms of foreign currency we have

$$BP = ePX - P_wM + K. \tag{7.2.2}$$

If *BP* in equation (7.2.2) is zero the inflow of foreign currency into the economy arising from both exports and capital inflows is exactly offset by the outflow of foreign currency arising from imports and capital outflows. What happens if *BP* is not equal to zero? If *BP* is negative, for example, more foreign currency is flowing out of the economy than coming in; we have a situation of excess demand for foreign currency. Under a regime of fixed exchange rates this excess demand will not affect the price of foreign currency, ie the exchange rate, and the question arises as to where the currency comes from or who supplies the excess demand?[1] The answer is that the excess demand is supplied from the foreign currency reserves of the central bank of the economy; call these *R*. Thus when the balance of payments is negative foreign currency reserves fall, and there is a balance of payments problem. Analogously, when the balance of payments is positive foreign currency reserves rise and there is balance of payments 'joy'.[2]

We shall define equilibrium in the international sector as a situation in which the balance of payments is zero, and thus a situation in which the change in foreign currency reserves is equal to zero. We define equilibrium in the international sector in this way because, given that most countries have only limited foreign currency reserves, we know that if the balance of payments is negative, and therefore reserves are falling, something will have to be done. The country involved will have to undertake some policy to change the balance of payments; hence the situation is not one that can be maintained.[3]

The above definition of equilibrium in the international sector involves a problem which for the most part we shall ignore. As we can see from equation (7.2.2) the balance of payments can be equal to zero even though there is a balance of trade deficit,

[1] As in all price-fixing situations, if the excess demand is not supplied either the fixed price will change or black markets will develop.

[2] As any surplus or deficit in the balance of payments is made up by changes in reserves the *ex post* 'balance of payments' is always zero. In equation (7.2.2) above, however, we do not include changes in reserves in *K* precisely because we want to examine when international transactions will affect the level of reserves.

[3] A situation in which the balance of payments is positive and therefore reserves are rising is less clearcut. A country could continue to accumulate reserves without undertaking any policies to change the balance of payments. For our purposes we could have defined equilibrium as a situation in which the balance of payments is zero or positive.

as long as net capital inflows are large enough to offset this deficit. However, net capital inflows mean that foreigners are acquiring domestic assets, ie claims to future domestic income streams. Thus in this situation residents are exchanging future income streams for current goods and services, ie they are borrowing. Clearly this situation will at some point have some effect on the constraints facing residents and therefore on their behaviour. However, with the definition of equilibrium given above this is considered an equilibrium situation. The reasons why we ignore this complication is that we are mainly interested in the short run and in the whole model presented previously we have ignored the effects of changes in wealth, and so continue to do so here.

7.3   The balance of payments and the domestic economy

In the first part of this chapter we examined how international trade affected the equilibrium values of domestic economic variables; income, the price level and the rate of interest. We can now examine how these domestic economic variables in turn affect equilibrium in the international sector, ie how the balance of payments is affected by these variables. The two components of the balance of payments are the balance of trade and net capital flows. We have already examined the determinants of the two components of the balance of trade, exports and imports, and assumed they are related to domestic disposable income and the domestic price level relative to that of the rest of the world. We must now turn to the determinants of net capital flows.

Capital flows occur when individuals are acquiring foreign assets. The reason why individuals acquire assets is because assets yield an income stream in the future. Therefore in choosing among assets individuals will compare their income streams and choose that asset which yields the highest rate of return, adjusted of course for risks, non-pecuniary yields, and so on.[1] We shall therefore postulate that international capital flows are a function of the relative rates of interest in the countries involved or, $K = f(\frac{r}{r_w})$

where r is the domestic rate of interest and r_w is the rate of interest in the rest of the world. If we assume that the rate of interest in the rest of the world is given, we have a direct relationship between the domestic rate of interest and net capital flows. The higher is the domestic rate of interest the higher will be capital inflows (foreigners now prefer to buy domestic assets) and the lower will be capital outflows (residents find foreign assets relatively less attractive). Adding this idea to the previous discussion about the determinants of the balance of payments we have the following,

$$BP = ePX(\frac{eP}{P_w}) - P_w M (\frac{eP}{P_w}, Y_D) + K (\frac{r}{r_w}). \qquad (7.3.1)$$

---

[1] See the discussion in chapter 3.

Equation (7.3.1) shows that the balance of payments is a function of domestic disposable income, the domestic price level, and the domestic rate of interest, *given* the world price level, the world interest rate, and the exchange rate. Following our previous discussion we assume that the balance of payments is negatively related to the first two of these and positively related to the third.

It is a little complicated to express diagrammatically a relationship like that shown by equation (7.3.1). However, in this case we have a very easy expedient. From our analysis of an economy in equilibrium at less than full employment, in which the money wage rate is fixed, we know that there is a unique positive relationship between the *equilibrium* real income and the *equilibrium* price level. We can see this in figure 7.3.1(b) where the equilibrium income and price level are shown by some points on the $W^o Y_f$ curve if the money wage rate is fixed at W^o and by some points on the $W' Y_f$ curve if it is fixed at $W' > W^o$. What these points will be depends, of course, on the position of the *EE* curve. As both the domestic price level and income affect the balance of payments in the same direction we can use the price level, by itself, to represent the effect of both of these on the balance of payments, because a rise, say, in the *equilibrium* price level is accompanied by a rise in equilibrium income, which affects the balance of payments in the same direction.[1] In figure 7.3.1(a) we measure the domestic price level on the vertical axis, and the rate of interest on the horizontal axis. The curves marked *BB* and $B'B'$ show all the combinations of the price level and interest rates for which we have balance of payments equilibrium; the former for a situation in which

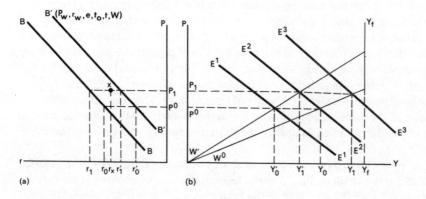

Figure 7.3.1

[1] Once we reach full employment (Y_f) or in an economy with flexible wages in which equilibrium income is always Y_f, changes in the price level are not accompanied by changes in real income. In these cases only changes in the price level are relevant for the balance of payments.

the fixed money wage rate in the domestic economy is W^o, the latter for a situation in which it is W'.

The derivation of these curves is quite straightforward. Assume that the *equilibrium* domestic price level is P_o and that the economy is characterized by the fixed money wage rate W^o. Equilibrium income in the economy is therefore Y_o (ie E^2E^2 is the relevant EE curve). This combination of domestic income and the domestic price level results in some level of imports and exports which results in some foreign currency flow, positive or negative. Find that rate of interest which will result in a net capital flow which will exactly offset the currency flow generated by the balance of trade, call it r_o. Thus the point $P_o r_o$ represents a situation in which net foreign currency flows are zero, which is exactly how we defined balance of payments equilibrium. If with the same fixed money wage rate the equilibrium domestic price level goes to P_1, because of a shift in the EE curve to the right (to E^3E^3), domestic real income rises to Y_1. The rise in the price level and in domestic income worsens the balance of trade, therefore to maintain balance of payments equilibrium net capital inflows must be greater, which will only occur if the interest rate is greater, say r_1. Thus the point $P_1 r_1$ also represents balance of payments equilibrium. We do this for every price level to derive the BB curve.

If the fixed money wage rate in the domestic economy rises to W' we can see that each equilibrium price level is associated with a lower real income. The equilibrium price level P_o is now associated with an equilibrium income level Y'_o, the equilibrium price level P_1 with an equilibrium income level Y'_1. As far as the balance of trade is concerned this means that each equilibrium price level is associated with a larger balance of trade (because a lower income implies lower imports), thus the net capital flow required to maintain balance of payments equilibrium is lower and therefore the domestic interest rate necessary to maintain balance of payments equilibrium is lower. In our example with the fixed money wage rate W', and the equilibrium price level P_o, the rate of interest required to maintain balance of payments equilibrium is r'_o; with the equilibrium price level P_1, a rate of interest of r'_1. Thus the curve marked $B'B'$ shows all the combinations of the price level and interest rate which will result in balance of payments equilibrium when the fixed money wage rate in the economy is W'.[1]

Before leaving the BB curve two points should be made explicit: first, the variables that are held constant along the BB curve; second, the forces generated in the system if the economy is off the BB curve, ie the balance of payments is not in equilibrium.

---

[1] Of course, as mentioned earlier (note 1, p. 115), if the economy is characterized by flexible money wages every price level is associated with the full employment level of income Y_f, and changes in the money wage rate do not affect the level of income and therefore the balance of payments. In this case the money wage rate is not held constant along the BB curve.

We saw above that if money wage rates are not flexible, changes in the fixed money wage rate change the *BB* curve. The reason for this is that we are using the price level not only to represent the relative price effect on the balance of trade, but also as a proxy for the income effect. However, the relationship between any equilibrium price level and the corresponding equilibrium income level depends on the fixed money wage rate. Thus the fixed money wage rate is held constant along the *BB* curve. We know from our whole discussion of the balance of payments that the world price level and the world rate of interest will affect the balance of trade and capital flows respectively, and therefore the balance of payments. Changes in these will therefore shift the *BB* curve.[1] We assumed that imports, the balance of trade and the balance of payments depend on real domestic disposable income (see equation 7.3.1, p. 114). Any level of real income can be associated with different levels of disposable income, given different levels of taxation. Therefore t_o and t, our two tax variables, are also held constant along the *BB* curve. In figure 7.3.1(a) assume that the curve marked *BB* is the relevant one for some given tax t_o. A rise in taxes to t_o^1, for example, means that for every equilibrium level of income, disposable income is lower, imports are lower and therefore the balance of trade is greater. The new balance of payments equilibrium curve will be $B'B'$. The final variable that is held constant along the *BB* curve is the exchange rate. We shall assume that a fall in the exchange rate, making foreign currency more expensive in terms of domestic currency, will lead to an increase in exports and a decrease in imports such that the net currency inflow arising from the balance of trade will improve, shifting the *BB* curve to the right. The variables held constant are shown in the parentheses in figure 7.3.1(a).

Any point off the *BB* curve shows a situation of balance of payments disequilibrium; any point above the *BB* curve shows a balance of payments deficit; any point below the *BB* curve shows a balance of payments surplus. Take point X in figure 7.3.1(a), and assume that this point represents equilibrium in the economy; the economy is in equilibrium with a price level P', some real income associated with that price level, and an interest rate of r_x. If the relevant balance of payments equilibrium curve is *BB*, point X represents a balance of payments deficit. We can see this in the following way. The *BB* curve shows that the necessary combination of the price level and interest rate to achieve balance of payments equilibrium is P' and r_1. The actual rate of interest in the economy is, by assumption, r_x, lower than r_1. Therefore the net capital flow is lower than that required to maintain balance of payments equilibrium, hence there is a balance of payments deficit. If the relevant balance of payments equilibrium curve is the one marked $B'B'$, point X represents a situation of balance of payments surplus by an analogous argument to that given above.

What forces are generated in the economy at a point like X? Under a fixed exchange

[1] A rise in the world price level or a fall in the world interest rate will shift the *BB* curve to the right.

system we know that in this situation foreign currency reserves are either falling or rising (depending on whether the relevant balance of payments equilibrium curve is *BB* or *B'B'*). With such a system the central bank, to maintain the exchange rate, must act as the buyer or seller of last resort in the foreign currency market. If it does not, the excess demand or supply of foreign currency will lead to a change in the exchange rate. Thus the initial force generated by a disequilibrium situation is on the level of foreign currency reserves held by the economy. The next question is whether this leads to a change in any of the other variables in the system. The answer is that clearly it does not. The values of the economic variables in the system — real income, the price level, the rate of interest — is the outcome of the interaction of the various behavioural functions we postulated, the consumption function, the investment function, the supply of labour, and so on. In none of these was the level of foreign currency reserves a relevant behavioural variable, so that changes in foreign currency reserves will not affect any of these functions, and therefore will not lead to any changes in the variables determined by these functions.[1]

The lack of any links to transmit changes in foreign currency reserves to changes in the other variables does not mean, however, that a balance of payments disequilibrium can continue without affecting the domestic economy. Given that no country has unlimited foreign currency reserves a continuous fall in reserves will force the country to undertake some economic policy that will improve the balance of payments. These policies will attempt to change some or all of the economic variables relevant to the balance of payments. It is via these policies that domestic variables will be affected.

To summarize: a balance of payments disequilibrium under a regime of fixed exchange rates has no direct effect on any domestic economic variables, but it does affect government policy; it is the change in government policy which then affects the other economic variables.

7.4   Internal and external equilibrium
In figure 7.4.1 below we incorporate the international sector into the model of the economy previously presented. The *EE* and *LL* curves are those we derived in figure 7.1.1 above and we have added to these the two balance of payments equilibrium curves *BB* and *B'B'*. Thus figure 7.4.1 is a summary of the complete model of an open economy, incorporating the real balance of trade in the *EE* and *LL* curves; and the condition for balance of payments equilibrium in the *BB* curves. Assume that the

---

[1] We are assuming here that changes in foreign currency reserves do not affect the supply of money in the economy, ie that the central bank automatically undertakes open market operations to offset any effect of foreign currency flows on the domestic money supply. If the central bank does allow changes in foreign currency reserves to affect the money supply we can treat this as a deliberate monetary policy the effects of which we examine in section 7.5 below.

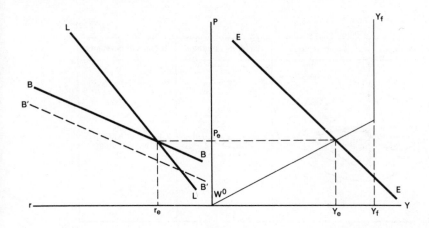

Figure 7.4.1

economy is in equilibrium with the price level at P_e, real income at Y_e, and the rate of interest at r_e. Assume also that the relevant balance of payments equilibrium curve is the one marked *BB*. In this case we have a situation of domestic equilibrium, for the given fixed money wage rate W_0, and balance of payments equilibrium. What if the relevant balance of payments equilibrium curve is the one marked $B'B'$? The equilibrium level of prices, income, and the rate of interest is still P_e, Y_e, and r_e respectively, as these are determined by the *EE* and *LL* curves, ie by the interaction of the goods, money, and employment sectors of the domestic economy. However, with the $B'B'$ curve this combination of the domestic variables results in a balance of payments deficit. In conjunction with the values of the other variables, the rate of interest is too low, and therefore net capital inflows are too low to yield balance of payments equilibrium.[1] In this situation foreign currency reserves start falling, and will continue to fall until the government undertakes some policy to change the situation.

Before examining the policy problems that arise in an open economy it will be useful to summarize schematically the open economy model developed above, just as we did with the closed economy models at the end of chapter 5. This is done not to bring out any new implications of the model, but to focus attention on the new links among the various sectors that are introduced in an open economy. The model presented in table 7.4.1 should be compared with model 3 in table 5.7.1 at the end of chapter 5; it is a fixed money wage model. The four columns of table 7.4.1 represent the four sectors into which we have subdivided the economy — the money sector, the goods sector, the

[1]Or, of course, in conjunction with the other variables the price level is too high and therefore the balance of trade is too low to yield balance of payments equilibrium.

Table 7.4.1

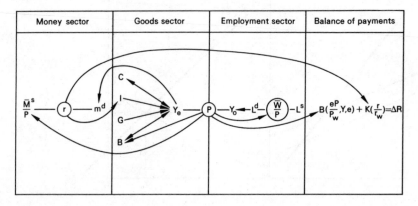

Money sector	Goods sector	Employment sector	Balance of payments

employment sector, and the balance of payments sector.[1] As before, the arrows
connecting the variables represent the links that transmit changes within and among
the sectors.

Looking at the money and goods sectors, we can see that the introduction of the
international sector does not introduce any new links between these. It is true that now
there is a link between the money sector and the balance of payments sector, via the
effect of the rate of interest on capital flows, but there are no links between capital
flows and the goods sector. Within the goods sector the introduction of the international
sector introduces two new links, one of which is of great importance to the analysis.
The less important one is that now there is a link between B and Y_e — the real balance
of trade affects the relationship between aggregate demand and the level of output.
This is a two-way link because we assumed that imports, one of the elements of the
balance of trade, are behaviourally dependent on the level of income. It is because of
this two-way link that the multiplier we obtained above (equation (7.1.7)) was different from the multiplier we had previously; the one in equation (7.1.7) incorporates
the marginal propensity to import (m_1). It will be recalled that the whole multiplier
analysis arises when some elements of desired expenditures are behaviourally dependent
on the level of real income, and therefore changes in these elements both affect the level
of output and are in turn affected by the level of output (see chapter 2). Before the
introduction of the international sector the only such element was consumption; now
it is both consumption and the balance of trade.

Analytically, the more important and more difficult new link is the one between

---

[1] In the goods sector we have also incorporated G — another element of aggregate demand —
discussed in chapter 6.

the price level and the balance of trade. This link arises from our assumption that both exports and imports are behaviourally dependent on the domestic price level relative to that of the rest of the world. It is this link which makes the *IS* curve, which is the equilibrium condition for the goods sector, depend on the price level; we examined the effect of this link in figure 7.1.1(a) above, where we had to draw different *IS* curves for different price levels. The importance of this link can be seen by re-examining one of the extreme cases we analyzed at the end of chapter 5 (figure 5.5.4). This was the situation where we assumed that investment did not depend on the rate of interest, and therefore the *EE* curve was perfectly inelastic. We examined the consequences of this assumption in a model of perfectly flexible prices and wages, and saw that if the *EE* curve was to the right of the $Y_f Y_f$ curve we would get continuous inflation. The reason for this was that the link between the price level and aggregate demand operated via the link between the money sector and the goods sector, ie the rate of interest; once this was broken there was no mechanism by which changes in the price level could be transmitted to changes in aggregate demand. If we look at table 7.4.1 we see that in an open economy a direct link exists between the price level and the goods sector. Thus changes in the price level can be transmitted to aggregate demand even if the link between the money sector and the goods sector were broken. Geometrically what this means is that in an open economy even if investment is not a function of the rate of interest the *EE* curve is downward-sloping.[1]

The other links in the table are quite straightforward. We can see the relationship between the balance of payments, which is equal to the change in foreign currency reserves (ΔR), and the other domestic variables, the balance of trade via Y_e and P and capital flows via the interest rate. We can also see the point discussed earlier that a change in foreign currency reserves does not by itself generate any force on any of the other variables in the system; there is no link from ΔR to any of the other sectors.

We saw above that disequilibrium in the balance of payments does not exert any force on any domestic economic variables and therefore there is no tendency for the disequilibrium to be cured. However, the change in the level of foreign currency reserves accompanied by the desire to maintain the fixed exchange rate will lead to some government policy aimed at solving the balance of payments problem. From the balance of payments equation,

$$BP = Pe\, X\!\left(\frac{eP}{P_w}\right) - P_w M\!\left(\frac{eP}{P_w},\, Y_D\right) + K\!\left(\frac{r}{r_w}\right) \qquad (7.4.1)$$

we can see that not all of the relevant variables are under the direct control of domestic

[1]It is a useful exercise to check this statement by deriving an *EE* curve directly from an *IS* curve which assumes that investment is not a function of the rate of interest.

economic policy. P, e, Y_D and r can be changed by the use of monetary and fiscal policy, as discussed in the last chapter, but P_w and r_w are not under the direct control of domestic policy-makers. We can also see that some of the relevant variables for the achievement of balance of payments goals are also relevant to the achievement of other economic goals. For example, an increase in domestic income and employment may be one of the goals of economic policy, irrespective of the balance of payments situation; a change in the rate of interest to increase the level of investment may also be a policy goal irrespective of the balance of payments situation. What this implies is that there may arise a conflict between the goal of attaining balance of payments equilibrium and other goals.

7.5   Monetary and fiscal policies

We shall first examine the use of general monetary and fiscal policies for balance of payments purposes. In figure 7.5.1 the solid lines represent some initial situation in an economy with equilibrium level of income, prices, and the rate of interest at Y_e, P_e, and r_e respectively. The dashed lines represent the new equilibrium after some policy has been put into effect. We can see that in the initial situation the economy has a balance of payments deficit. From our analysis of government policy in the last chapter we know that both monetary and fiscal policies can be depicted by a shift in the EE and LL curves. A contractionary fiscal policy (whether an increase in taxes or a decrease in expenditures) is shown by a shift to the left of the EE curve and a shift to the right of the LL curve; a contractionary monetary policy is shown by a shift to the left of both the EE and LL curves. The former lowers income, prices, and the rate of interest; the latter has the same effect on income and prices, but raises the rate of interest. From our discussion of the BB curve, we know that a change in monetary policy or in government expenditures will not affect it, but a change in taxes will.[1] The problem facing the policy-maker is therefore as follows: given the deficit in the balance of payments depicted in figure 7.5.1, find some monetary or fiscal policy (or a combination of the two) which will lead to that combination of income, the price level, and the rate of interest such that equilibrium in the domestic economy is associated with balance of payments equilibrium. Or in terms of our geometric representation of the economy, to find a policy such that in equilibrium the LL curve intersects the BB curve.

In figure 7.5.1 we have depicted a situation in which both a contractionary monetary and expenditure policy are effective in solving the balance of payments deficit there depicted.[2] Using expenditure policy the new equilibrium situation is Y_F, P_F and r_F;

---

[1] Changes in monetary policy or in government expenditures will result in a movement along the BB curve. The variables held constant along the BB curve (see figure 7.3.1) are P_w, r_w, e, t_0, t and W.

[2] Whether a contractionary or expansionary fiscal policy is necessary to curb the balance of

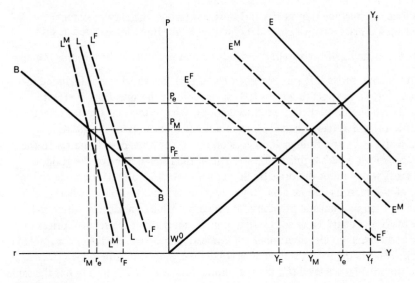

Figure 7.5.1

using monetary policy it is at Y_M, P_M, and r_M. We can see that when the balance of payments problem is solved with the use of expenditure policy the equilibrium level of domestic income, and the price level, are lower than when it is solved with the use of monetary policy. This should not be surprising. A contractionary expenditure policy reduces income, prices, and the rate of interest; a fall in income and prices affects the balance of trade favourably, a fall in the rate of interest affects net capital flows unfavourably. On the other hand a contractionary monetary policy reduces income and prices but increases the rate of interest; all its effects are thus favourable to the balance of payments and therefore income and prices do not have to fall by as much to solve the balance of payments problem.[1]

7.6 Tariffs and subsidies
We now turn to two specific balance of payments policies in general use, namely import tariffs and export subsidies. A casual glance at the balance of payments equation (7.4.1)

payments problem depends on the relative effect of the policy on prices and income on the one hand and the interest rate on the other. In terms of the figure it depends on the relative slopes of the *BB* and *LL* curves.

[1] A change in taxes can be analyzed in the same way as a change in expenditures, except that a change in taxes will also lead to a shift of the *BB* curve. It is a useful exercise to examine what is the best combination of monetary and fiscal policies if one wants to solve a balance of payments problem while at the same time to achieve a higher level of domestic income.

may lead one to conclude that tariffs and subsidies have no balance of payments effects, as they do not seem to enter the equation at all. However, as soon as one examines the meaning of the variable $\frac{eP}{P_w}$ and the reason for its inclusion, this impression will be quickly revised. It will be remembered that this variable was included in both the import and export functions to take account of the substitution effect between foreign and domestically produced goods. What is relevant for this effect is the effective price that has to be paid by the ultimate consumer of the goods in question. If the price of a foreign good goes up by 20 per cent, does it matter to the domestic consumer whether this is due to a rise in the foreign price of the good, or due to a tariff which raises the price by 20 per cent? Analogously, if the price to the foreigner of a domestic good falls by 20 per cent, does it matter to him whether this fall is due to a fall in domestic prices by 20 per cent or due to a subsidy which reduces the price by 20 per cent? Thus both tariffs and subsidies affect the relative prices of domestic and foreign goods, the former for domestic importers, the latter for foreign importers. As far as the balance of trade is concerned, a tariff has the same effect as a change in the world price level (P_w) in the import function, and a subsidy has the same effect as a change in the domestic price level in the *export function*.[1]

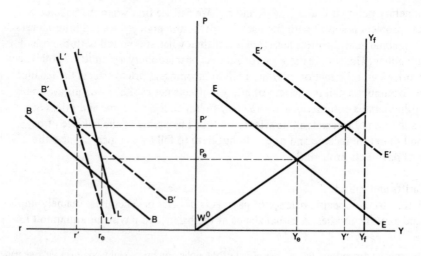

Figure 7.6.1

<hr />

[1] If one takes account of tariffs and subsidies the relative price of imports is $\frac{eP}{P_{w(1+t)}}$ where t is a per cent tariff, the relative price of exports is $\frac{eP(1-s)}{P_w}$ where s is a per cent subsidy.

We use figure 7.6.1 below to show the effects of tariffs and subsidies. The solid lines represent some initial situation in an economy with equilibrium level of income, prices, and the rate of interest at Y_e, r_e, and P_e respectively. The dashed lines represent the new equilibrium after a tariff or subsidy. In the initial situation the economy has a balance of payments deficit; the point $P_e r_e$ at which the domestic economy is in equilibrium is not on the *BB* curve. Assume that a tariff or a subsidy is introduced. What is the effect of this on all the relevant variables? The post tariff or subsidy (or both) situation is shown by the curves marked $E'E'$, $L'L'$, and $B'B'$. The new equilibrium is one with a higher income, higher prices, and a higher rate of interest. Let us examine the economics underlying the above geometry.

The effect of the tariff or subsidy is to decrease imports or increase exports, and thus increase the real balance of trade. Aggregate demand on domestic resources is increased. An increase in aggregate demand arising from a change in the goods sector (a shift in the *IS* curve) is shown in our model by a shift to the right of the *EE* curve and a shift to the left of the *LL* curve. As we saw above, a tariff can be viewed as a change in the world price level to importers, and a subsidy as a change in the domestic price level to exporters; thus they shift the *BB* curve upwards.[1]

We can look at the tariff or subsidy as a combination of an expansionary fiscal policy (the shift in the *EE* and *LL* curves) accompanied by a change in the balance of payments equilibrium condition (the change in the *BB* curve).[2] The expansionary fiscal policy improves the balance of payments insofar as it raises the interest rate, and worsens the balance of payments insofar as it raises prices and income (see note 2, p. 122). The change in the balance of payments equilibrium condition induced by the tariff or subsidy improves the balance of payments. The net effect of this policy on the balance of payments, therefore, depends on the relative size of the various effects.

7.7   Devaluation

The analysis of tariffs and subsidies in the last sector can easily be extended to examine the effects of a devaluation. The relative price of foreign and domestic goods depends not only on foreign and domestic price levels but also on the exchange rate. It is because of this, of course, that the relative price variable we used in both the import

[1] Whether a subsidy shifts the *BB* curve up or down depends on the elasticity of demand for exports. The foreign currency inflow generated by exports (F_x) equals ePX and $\frac{\partial F_x}{\partial P} = e[P\frac{dX}{dP} + X]$ $= eX[\eta x + 1] \gtreqless 0$ as $|\eta x| \lesseqgtr 1$.

[2] We can therefore use the same analysis to analyze the effects of the following: a rise in the world price level, a fall in the world interest rate accompanied by an expansionary fiscal policy, a reduction in foreign tariffs.

and export functions was $\frac{eP}{P_w}$ (see note 2, p. 109). The price of foreign goods to

importers in terms of domestic currency is $\frac{P_w}{e}$; the price of domestic goods to

foreigners in terms of their currency is eP. A fall in the exchange rate thus makes foreign goods more expensive to residents and domestic goods cheaper to foreigners. The effects of this on exports and imports are the same as a combination of a tariff and a subsidy (at the same rate) on all traded goods. We can thus use figure 7.6.1 to show all the effects of a devaluation. Let the curves marked *EE, LL* and *BB* represent the pre-devaluation situation and those marked $E'E'$, $L'L'$, and $B'B'$ the post-devaluation situation. As with tariffs and subsidies the net effect of the devaluation on the balance of payments depends on the relative magnitudes of the various effects involved. The expansionary effects of the rise in exports and fall in imports raises income, the price level and the rate of interest. The first two would tend to worsen the balande of payments, the last to improve it. The shift in the *BB* curve would tend to improve the balance of payments. The net effect is thus ambiguous.

Before leaving this chapter one point should be noted. We have discussed the problems raised by the introduction of international transactions mainly in the context of a fixed money wage model. This was done because that is the most difficult of the models we have examined; changes in the price level are accompanied by changes in income and therefore income effects cannot be ignored. All of the analysis we did can easily be carried out in a model of flexible wages in which income is always at the full employment level. In such a model there are no income effects to worry about, and one need only look at the price and interest rate effects of international transactions.

references

FLEMING J Marcus 'Domestic Financial Policies Under Fixed and Under Flexible Exchange Rates' *Canadian Journal of Economics and Political Science* 1964 vol. 30 pp. 421 - 30.
JOHNSON H G 'Theoretical Problems of the International Monetary System' in R N Cooper (ed.) *International Finance* Penguin Modern Economics Readings 1971.
MUNDELL R A 'The Appropriate Use of Monetary and Fiscal Policy for Internal and External Stability' IMF Staff Papers 1962, vol. 9 pp. 70 - 79.
– 'Capital Mobility and Stabilization Policy Under Fixed and Flexible Exchange Rates' *Canadian Journal of Economics and Political Science* 1964, vol. 30 pp. 421 - 30.

chapter 8

application and extensions of the analysis

In the last seven chapters we constructed a model of an economy, ie a framework within which to analyze the interrelationships among various types of economic decisions, and the forces generated by them. We used very simple behavioural assumptions to exemplify the model and, more important, to show how, via such assumptions, links are created among and within the different sectors of decision-making. However, what we have done is only a first step in trying to understand the complexities of an economy. The general purpose of this, the final chapter, is to indicate where one goes from here. We start by looking at how the model can be extended and modified and put to work. This is to emphasize, once again, that the purpose of a model, such as the one presented in this book, for example, is not only to present a particular set of assumptions about behaviour. Rather it is to provide a framework of analysis to be used to trace out the implications of many different types of assumptions. A model is to be conceived of as a tool for the analysis of problems. As with all tools it takes practice to know when and how to use them well. This idea is explored with reference to changing assumptions about the determinants of consumption behaviour (section 8.2). In the last seven chapters we have stated many hypotheses about behaviour. However, we have nowhere confronted these hypotheses with the 'real world'. Is observed consumer behaviour consistent with the assumption that consumption depends on current income? Do changes in the rate of interest lead to changes in investment? Do changes in income and the rate of interest lead to changes in the demand for money? Such questions can only be answered by observing actual behaviour; for example, by looking at the actual relationship between consumption and income over time or across different income groups. To see how some of these questions are answered we examine some of the empirical work that has been done on one of the behavioural relationships we used in our model – the consumption function (section 8.2). It is not intended to present an exhaustive summary of the vast amount of empirical work that has been done on this relationship. The intention is to give some of the flavour of how theory and empirical work interact; how the theory points out what aspects of the 'real world' are significant for a particular problem, and how the resulting empirical work leads to the modification of the theory or to its rejection.

The last three sections of this chapter move into an area we have only touched on previously. What we have done is comparative statics. We compared an equilibrium situation after some change had occurred with the equilibrium situation before the change. Such a framework is not very conducive to problems whose essential elements involve the path of variables over time; adjustments to discrepancies between desired and actual values of certain variables; expectations about an imperfectly perceived future and adjustments to such expectations. Within such a framework it is difficult to examine some problems, for example growth, business cycles and inflation. Yet these problems are important. We first show how we can take some tentative steps in the direction of a theory of growth (section 8.3) and business cycles (section 8.4) by connecting investment with the capital stock and the capital stock with output. We then go on to examine inflation (section 8.5) which, especially when accompanied by unemployment, remains one of the most troublesome problems of current economic theory.

8.1   The consumption function (1)

When we discussed consumption (chapter 2) we assumed that the consumption function was of the form

$$C = F(Y), \tag{8.1.1}$$

ie consumption was a function of current income. We then modified it to make it a function of disposable income, but this modification does not matter for our present purposes. Assume now that somebody suggests that a better theory is that consumption depends not only on current income but also on physical wealth, or

$$C = F(Y, W) \tag{8.1.2}$$

where W represents physical wealth. A superficial, mechanical knowledge of the model presented previously may lead one to conclude that it cannot handle this new theory, because the model 'assumed' that consumption was a function of income. Clearly this would be wrong. What the model did was trace out the implication of a relationship between consumption and income, or what links within and among the various sectors such a relationship creates. As the second theory of consumption also assumes a relationship between consumption and income it implies the same sort of links as the first. The second theory might give us a better understanding of the determinants of consumption; it might imply a different value for the relationship between consumption and income, and it implies that changes in wealth shift the consumption function (as specified by equation (8.1.1)). But the links in the model were not dependent on any particular value of the parameters, therefore changes in these do not affect the links, though they will affect the quantitative effect of a change in any one variable on the others.

Assume now that it is suggested that a still better understanding of consumption is obtained if we assume that consumption depends not only on real physical wealth but also on the real quantity of money, ie

$$C = F\left(Y, W, \frac{M^s}{P}\right). \tag{8.1.3}$$

This seems a much more complicated relationship than the one of equation (8.1.1). How can we handle it? The assumption of equation (8.1.3) introduces two links we did not have before: a link between the nominal money supply (M^s) and consumption, and a link between the price level and consumption. The link between the price level and consumption means that the goods sector of the economy, of which consumption is an element, depends on the price level, therefore equilibrium in the goods sector depends on the price level. Given that the *IS* curve summarizes equilibrium in the goods sector of the economy, it will also depend on the price level. However, this is nothing new. When we introduced the real balance of trade into our model (chapter 7), and assumed that it depended on the price level, we analyzed the effect of such a link. The only added complication introduced by the consumption function of the form shown by equation (8.1.3) is that changes in the nominal quantity of money, for a given price level, also affect consumption and therefore equilibrium in the goods sector ie the *IS* curve. Thus changes in the supply of money affect both the *LM* and the *IS* curves.

Let us look at a slightly more complicated example. It is suggested that consumption depends not only on real physical wealth but also on the quantity of financial wealth, which we shall assume is composed of the real quantity of money and the real quantity of government bonds outstanding, ie

$$C = F\left(Y, \frac{M}{P}, \frac{B_g}{P}\right), \tag{8.1.4}$$

where $\frac{B_g}{P}$ represents the real quantity of government bonds in the economy. At first glance it may seem that the introduction of government bonds into the consumption function does not affect the links in the model of the economy discussed earlier. The quantity of government bonds did not appear in any of our previous behavioural functions and therefore changes in these should not introduce any new links into our model.[1]

A more careful analysis will show that this conclusion is not valid. It is true that we did not introduce the quantity of government bonds explicitly into any of our

---

[1] See, however, the discussion in the appendix to chapter 6.

behavioural functions. However, when we examined the budget constraint of the government (chapter 6, p. 97) we saw that the government could not change one of its policy variables (taxes, government expenditures, or the quantity of money) without affecting some other variable in its budget constraint. Until the introduction of the consumption function specified by equation (8.1.4) we could logically examine the effects of any government policy taken alone by assuming that the corresponding change, necessitated by the budget constraint, would occur in the quantity of government bonds outstanding. As the quantity of government bonds did not appear explicitly in any of the behavioural functions in our model, the net effect of the policy change would be that shown by the explicit change of the policy variable under study. If we introduce the consumption function shown by equation (8.1.4) this is no longer the case. Every variable in the government budget constraint now appears in some behavioural function in the model. And as every policy change involves a change in at least two of the variables in the government budget constraint, there are at least two links via which every government policy affects the economy.

The above discussion should make it clear that the model of the economy developed in the first seven chapters of the book is much more flexible, and therefore potentially more useful, than may appear at first sight; or, what is more important, that the simple behavioural assumptions used to illustrate a model do not constrain it to the analysis of only those assumptions.

8.2   The consumption function (II)

There has probably been more empirical work done on the consumption function than on any other behavioural relationship in economics. The work over the last thirty years or so shows clearly how theory and empirical work modify each other to rationalize observed behaviour. In the empirical work on the consumption function (and other economic relationships) two types of data have been used; family budget studies which examine the relationship between consumption and income among different income groups at some point of time (cross-section studies), and time series studies which analyze the relationship between consumption and income over time.[1] The early studies of the consumption function, which relied mainly on cross-section data, seemed to conform well with a consumption function of the form we used in our model,

---

[1] For the following discussion it is important to understand the difference in these two types of study. Assume we wish to examine the relationship between consumption and income. In time-series studies we look at the pairs $(C_1, Y_1), (C_2, Y_2) - (C_t, Y_t)$ where C and Y refer to aggregate consumption and aggregate income respectively (ie for the whole economy), and the indices 1, 2, $- t$ refer to time periods. In cross-section studies we look at the pairs $(C_1, Y_1), (C_2, Y_2) - (C_n, Y_n)$ where Y refers to the average income of a particular income group, C refers to the average consumption of the particular group. For example, Y_1 may be the average income of the income group £1,000 - £1,200 per annum and C_1 the average consumption of that income group.

ie $C = a + b \ Y$, in which the average propensity to consume $\frac{C}{Y} = \frac{a}{Y} + b$, falls as income
rises. However, new evidence soon cast doubt on this formulation. Time-series studies
made by Kuznets using data over the period 1869-1929 for the US showed that the
ratio of consumption to income over this period did not change even though income
had quadrupled; budget studies carried out in different periods with widely differing
average incomes showed great similarity in the overall average propensity to consume,
even though each one individually showed a declining average propensity to consume
as predicted by the hypothesis. Evidence of the consumption-income ratio over the
cycle was also not favourable to the simple consumption function. During minor
recessions consumption falls very slightly and sometimes continues to rise even though
income is decreasing.

The various pieces of evidence, which seemed to be contradictory in terms of the
consumption function specified by equation (8.1.1) above, stimulated theoretical
development aimed at explaining the observed characteristics of consumer behaviour.
All the new theories had to at least reconcile the discrepancy between the time series
and the cross-section data, ie why in the latter the average propensity to consume
declined as income rose while in the former it remained constant. One of the first
attempts to do this was made by Duesenberry in his relative income hypothesis. There
are two strands to this hypothesis. First, that the ratio of consumption to income is
not determined by the absolute income of an individual but by his position in the
income distribution, ie his relative income (his income relative to other income
recipients), and as one moves up the income distribution the ratio of consumption to
income falls. Second, that the individual's consumption also depends on his income
relative to his highest previous income, ie consumption patterns are not reversible over
time or at least they are difficult to reverse. The first strand of the relative income
hypothesis can be used to reconcile the different results found in time-series and cross-
section data. In the budget studies, families with different incomes and therefore in
different positions in the income distribution are examined. Here, according to
Duesenberry's hypothesis, one would expect that the higher is an individual's position
in the income distribution the lower will be his ratio of consumption to income, ie the
lower would be his average propensity to consume. However, over time, as all income
increases but the income distribution does not change, the consumption income ratio
does not change. Thus we would expect that time-series data would yield a constant
consumption income ratio.

The second strand of the hypothesis is used to rationalize the cyclical behaviour of
consumption. We can see this most clearly by using a very strong version of the
hypothesis. Assume that, within some range of income variation, consumption relationships are totally irreversible. If current income is below previous peak income (call this
Y_H) then consumption depends only on the previous peak income; if current income

is above previous peak income then consumption depends only on current income. The relationship between consumption and income over the cycle predicted by this theory is shown in figure 8.2.1 where we measure consumption and income on the vertical axis and time on the horizontal axis. Y_H^0, Y_H^1, and Y_H^2 are successive peak incomes occurring in periods t^0, t^1, and t^2 respectively. As income falls from Y_H^0 consumption is maintained at the level determined by Y_H^0, (and therefore $\frac{C}{Y}$ rises) until period t_0^0

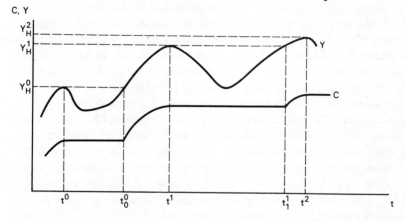

Figure 8.2.1

when current income again reaches Y_H^0. From then on, as income continues to rise consumption starts rising until the next peak income is reached in period t^1. As income falls from this new peak consumption remains stable until income again starts rising above this peak. Thus by introducing previous peak income as one of the determinants of consumption, ie by assuming that consumption relationships are not reversible (or just very sticky) we can rationalize the cyclical movements in $\frac{C}{Y}$

We can also use figure 8.2.1 to see how the relative income hypothesis of consumption modifies some of the analysis of the economy we carried out previously on the assumption that consumption depends only on the level of current income. In the extreme form in which it is presented in figure 8.2.1 we can see that between periods t^0 and t_0^0, t^1 and t_1^1 the marginal propensity to consume is zero. This means that the multiplier is unity. Therefore during that part of the cycle in which the level of current income is still below the previous peak income, government policy tends to be less effective than otherwise. This is, of course, not very surprising. As soon as current income becomes relatively unimportant for current expenditure decisions, changes in current income have little effect on expenditure decisions, and this after all is the whole basis for the multiplier analysis.

Another attempt at reconciling the evidence from the cross-section and time-series data was to postulate that consumption depends not only on current income but also on the level of wealth. For a given level of income, the higher is the level of wealth the higher is consumption and therefore the higher is the consumption income ratio. However, for a given level of wealth, a rise in income will lower the consumption income ratio as predicted by the simple hypothesis represented by equation (8.1.1) above. The way this hypothesis reconciles the cross-section and time-series evidence is to argue that in the time series we observe changes in consumption due to changes in income *and* in wealth (because wealth rises over time), while in the cross-section studies we observe changes in consumption due to changes in income only. In figure 8.2.2, we measure income on the horizontal axis and consumption on the vertical axis. Assume that the line through the origin marked C_t represents the relationship between consumption and income, as shown by the time-series data, with a constant average propensity to consume. The two lines marked C_1 and C_2 represent two consumption functions derived from cross-section data taken at two different periods of time: C_1 at a period when the level of wealth was W_1, and C_2 when it was W_2 greater than W_1. Each one of these functions shows a declining average propensity to consume: when income rises from Y_1 to Y_2 consumption would rise to A if the level of wealth remained at W_1 (the result we get in cross-section studies); however, if wealth were to rise to W_2 at the same time, consumption would rise to B.

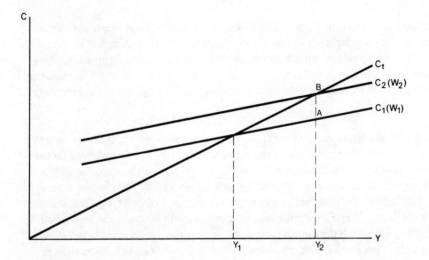

Figure 8.2.2

Both the theories examined above have a theme in common; one which has become increasingly important in theories which attempt to rationalize not only consumption but many other types of economic behaviour. The common theme is the idea that currently observed economic behaviour is not related only to current economic events; that in their economic decisions individuals take account of both current economic phenomena and past events. Or to put it another way, the relevant economic information on which decisions are made is supplied not only by the economic events that occur today but also by the economic events that have occurred in the past. In Duesenberry's theory it was past consumption decisions impinging on current consumption decisions. In the various wealth hypotheses it is past decisions about saving, which after all determine the current level of wealth, that impinge on current consumption.

If the past impinges on the present why should not the future do the same? If in deciding how much to consume today individuals take account of how much they have consumed yesterday, why should they not take account of how much they will be able to consume tomorrow? Of course, one may argue that the future is not as well known as the past. This is true. Nevertheless, we do observe that individuals, in many areas of decision-making, do behave as if they did have expectations about the occurrence of particular events. People save, presumably on the basis of some expectation that they or their heirs will exist in the future; people invest in a particular type of machine, presumably on the basis of some expectation that the goods produced by it will still be desirable in the future; people devote time and effort to acquiring certain skills, presumably on the basis of some expectation that these will be useful in the future. Of course these expectations may turn out to be wrong. That, however, is not the issue. The issue is whether, when constructing models which attempt to rationalize economic behaviour, we should assume that individuals consider the future as a complete unknown, or on the other hand whether we should assume that individuals do form some expectations about the future; that these expectations affect their behaviour in the present and that somehow this should be incorporated into our explanatory model.

The permanent income hypothesis developed by Milton Friedman in his *The Theory of the Consumption Function* is an attempt to provide a link between presently observed behaviour, the past, *and* the future. The concepts underlying the permanent income hypothesis are very simple to state. Such a statement, however, covers up the great ingenuity involved in transforming them into statements with empirical implications. It is only via such a transformation that theoretical constructs can be linked to observable phenomena, and these in turn used to test the theory.

Following Friedman, let us define permanent income as the income an individual expects to receive on the basis of such factors as his wealth, his occupation, his abilities, and all the other factors which are relevant to the acquisition of income. Some of the factors which determine the individual's permanent income might relate to the individual's past experience, for example his past income. Some of the factors may, however, be related to the experience of other similarly situated individuals. For example, if an individual enters a particular profession he may take account of the earnings of the members of that profession at different stages in their careers in determining his permanent income. Thus permanent income is a very broad concept which attempts to take account of both the past and the expected future. Similarly, permanent consumption is that consumption which an individual expects (plans) to undertake. Transitory income and transitory consumption are the differences between actual (measured) income and permanent income, and actual (measured) consumption and permanent consumption respectively. These components arise from unexpected events. For example, an unexpected bad harvest will result in a negative transitory component of income; an unexpected illness will result in a positive transitory component in consumption.

The permanent income hypothesis has two aspects to it. First, it states that permanent consumption is some fraction of permanent income independent of permanent income (although possibly depending on other variables). Thus the average propensity to consume, in terms of the permanent concepts, is independent of income. Second, it assumes the following relationships between the various transitory elements: there is zero correlation between the permanent and the transitory elements of both income and consumption, and more important there is zero correlation between the transitory element of consumption and that of income. The way in which the permanent income hypothesis attempts to reconcile the conflicting evidence about consumption behaviour is to show that the relationship between permanent income, the true determinant of consumption, and measured income, the variable used in empirical work, is different in different situations. It is this difference that leads to the conflict. Once this difference is reconciled the conflict disappears.

This idea can be illustrated in figure 8.2.3.[1] Assume that the line $C = a + bY$ is the consumption function derived from a budget study of a large group of individuals with various income levels. Some individuals with a low income Y_0 are observed to consume $Y_0 A$, those with an average income $\bar{Y}$ consume $\bar{Y}C$ and those with a high income Y^1 consume $Y^1 E$, where Y_0, $\bar{Y}$, and Y^1 represent their measured income. Assume now that we get the following information. The permanent income of the group whose measured income is Y_0 is Y^p_0, that of the group whose income is $\bar{Y}$ is $\bar{Y}$, and that of the group whose income is Y^1 is Y^1_p. The relationship between measured consumption and permanent income is shown by the line BCD. The results shown by the line ACE occur only because the relationship between measured income and permanent income is different for the three income groups under consideration. For the low income groups permanent income is above measured income, for the high income groups permanent

---

[1] This figure is taken from M. Friedman, *The Theory of the Consumption Function* p.34.

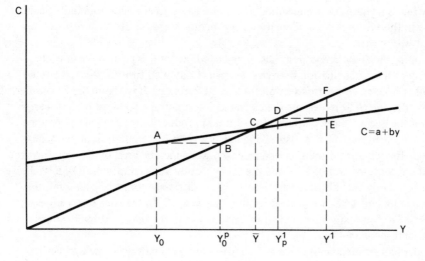

Figure 8.2.3

income is below measured income while for the average income group permanent and measured incomes are the same. Once we take account of this difference we get the 'true' consumption function.

Until now we assumed that the information about the relationship between measured income and permanent income was supplied to us. Is there any reason to believe that in budget studies the relationship will be that shown in the figure? The answer is yes. In every measured income group there are three types of individuals. There are those whose measured income represents their permanent income. In other words, their measured income does not include any transitory element, either positive or negative. Then there are those whose measured income is above their true permanent income; their measured income includes a positive transitory element. Lastly there are those whose measured income is below their permanent income; it includes a negative transitory element. Take the group represented by the measured income Y^1 in figure 8.2.3. As this is a 'high' income group it is more likely that it will include a higher proportion of individuals whose permanent income is below Y^1 and who are in this measured income group only because their transitory income is positive. After all, the individuals in this group were chosen exactly because their income is 'high' relative to the average income of all the groups ($\bar{Y}$). For an average income group like $\bar{Y}$ it is just as likely that it includes as many individuals who are there because their transitory component of income was positive as those for whom the transitory component was negative. Therefore this measured income might represent permanent income. As far as the low income group Y_0 is concerned, it is more likely to contain more individuals who are in this group because their transitory income was negative than of those for whom it was positive.

Of course the above hypothesis has to be tested. But if it is correct we have the beginning of the reconciliation between the results obtained from time-series studies and those obtained from cross-section studies. Referring back to figure 8.2.3 consider now that the line *BCD* represents the consumption function produced by time-series data, and the line *ACE* the consumption function produced by budget data. Assume also that in time-series data, measured income is a good representation of permanent income.[1] The problem is then to reconcile why at an income level of Y^1, say, the time series show consumption of Y^1F and the budget studies consumption of Y^1E. Well, we have done exactly that above. Even though we think we are comparing consumption at the same income level, we are not really doing so at all. In the time series a measured income of Y^1 represents a permanent income of Y^1, in the budget studies it represents a permanent income of only Y_p^1.

The permanent income hypothesis also offers an explanation for the cyclical behaviour of consumption. Short-term changes in measured income do not necessarily affect permanent income, especially if these are expected and therefore already incorporated in the decisions about consumption. Thus, according to the permanent income hypothesis, we would not expect consumption to move over the cycle with movements in income. In fact for mild cycles we might expect consumption to continue rising, say, even though measured income had fallen slightly.[2]

8.3   Investment and growth

Investment expenditures represent one of the most volatile elements of total expenditures. The simple behavioural hypothesis that the rate of interest is the major determinant of investment is not adequate to rationalise this phenomenon. One of the first steps to modify the simple hypothesis was to relate desired investment to changes in income. With this modification the investment function would be $I=f(\Delta Y, r)$, where ΔY is the change in income. There are various ways to rationalize the above assumption

---

[1] In time-series studies we look at the aggregate income of all individuals; it is therefore more likely that transitory elements will cancel out. Even in time series studies some transitory element, for example a business cycle, might affect all individuals in the same way, and therefore measured income might not be a correct measure of permanent income.

[2] Our discussions of the various hypotheses of consumption have been, necessarily, very brief. For an elaboration on such questions as; how is permanent income to be measured in the permanent income hypothesis? What forms of wealth are to be included in the wealth hypothesis? And most important how is one to choose among these various hypotheses? The reader is referred to M. Friedman, *The Theory of the Consumption Function*, and, for a more recent econometric analysis of the various theories, Michael K. Evans, *Macroeconomic Activity* chapters 2 and 3.

about desired investment. We shall look at one version of a whole set of hypotheses known as the stock adjustment principle.

The first step is to look at the capital stock as the ultimate object of decision-making rather than investment. The idea behind this step is quite simple. Labour and capital are the factors of production used by firms in producing their output. The firms' decision problems are how to allocate factors optimally in producing a particular level of output, and what level of output to produce. Thus both the level of output and the relative price of factors of production will be relevant to the firm's decisions about the quantity of factors it wants to have. Investment (net) is the act of changing the quantity of the capital stock, if it is not at the desired level. Therefore once a decision has been made about the desired level of the capital stock, this might also imply a decision about the amount of investment to be undertaken, but the relationship is not necessarily one to one (see below).

Following the above ideas, let us assume that there is a relationship $K = vY$ (8.3.1) between the stock of capital (K) and the level of output (Y), where $v = \dfrac{K}{Y}$, is the capital output ratio, ie it measures the number of units of capital required to produce one unit of output. It is not necessary, of course, to consider v itself as fixed, ie determined by technology alone. It may depend on other factors, for example the relative price of capital and the other factors of production. In that case v can be considered as the desired capital output ratio. However, to bring out the implication of this line of development most simply, let us assume that v is given. We can see right away that the level of output is relevant to the desired capital stock. What about investment?

We saw above that net investment can be looked at as the process of changing the capital stock from its actual level to a desired level. However, it is not necessary to assume that such changes will be made in a single time period, as it might take time to adjust the capital stock to its desired level. In general therefore we have

$$I_t = \delta \ (\overset{*}{K_t} - K_t). \tag{8.3.2}$$

where I_t is investment in period t, $\overset{*}{K_t}$, and K_t are the desired and the actual capital stock in period t respectively, and δ is the coefficient which measures what proportion of the discrepancy between the desired and the actual capital stock will be changed in the period. If δ is unity the whole discrepancy will be made up in one period; if it is less than unity only part of the discrepancy will be made up during the current period. For simplicity let us assume that it is unity. From equation (8.3.1) we have $\overset{*}{K_t} = vY_t$, ie the desired capital stock in period t will depend on the output in period t. What about K_t? Given that we have assumed that the capital stock is always fully adjusted within a period then the actual capital stock in period t is that stock which people desired in the previous period which is, using equation (8.3.1) again, vY_{t-1}.

We thus have

$$I_t = v\,(Y_t - Y_{t-1}) \text{ or } I_t = v\,\Delta Y_t . \tag{8.3.3}$$

Thus starting from the idea that the desired capital stock depends on the level of output we conclude that investment depends on the change in output. The relationship shown by equation (8.3.3) is called the accelerator principle. It states that investment is sensitive to changes in income. It is positive only if income is rising ($\Delta Y > 0$); zero when income is constant ($\Delta Y = 0$), and negative when income is falling ($\Delta Y < 0$). Moreover, even if income is growing, a change in the *rate* of growth of income will change investment. Thus a slowing down of the rate of growth of income will lead to an *absolute* fall in the level of investment.

The above investment relationship can easily be combined with the multiplier analysis to produce very elementary theories of growth and business cycles. Assume that consumption and investment are the only types of expenditures and that the consumption function is of the form $C = bY$. The equilibrium condition for the goods sector is $Y = C+I$, and substituting in the consumption relationship and rearranging we have $Y = \frac{1}{1-b} I$, or $Y = \frac{I}{s}$ where $s = 1 - b$ (the marginal propensity to save). Using this relationship and the accelerator relationship specified by equation (8.3.3) above we have

$$Y = \frac{v}{s}\Delta Y \text{ or } \frac{\Delta Y}{Y} = \frac{s}{v}. \tag{8.3.4}$$

Equation (8.3.4) represents the rate of growth of income in terms of v, the capital output ratio, and s, the saving ratio. Two equilibrium conditions are satisfied if income grows at the rate shown by this equation. We have equilibrium in the goods market, ie $Y = C + I$ at all points on this growth path, and the capital stock is growing at the same rate as output so that the ratio of capital to output is always v. We can see the latter point very simply in the following way. The rate of growth of the capital stock is $\frac{\Delta K}{K} = \frac{I}{K}$. Substituting $I = v\,\Delta Y$ and $K = vY$, we have $\frac{\Delta K}{K} = \frac{v\,\Delta Y}{vY} = \frac{\Delta Y}{Y}$. Assume now that: we start off with an economy at full employment with a growing population and therefore a growing labour force. Equation (8.3.4) above says that income will grow at some rate determined by the capital output ratio (which we are assuming fixed), and the saving ratio. This raises the question whether full employment can be maintained along the growth path and what happens to per capita income along the growth path.

Assume that the population and the labour force grow at the rate n. Let us examine the three possibilities, $n = \frac{s}{v}$, $n > \frac{s}{v}$, and $n < \frac{s}{v}$. In the first case the rate of population growth is equal to the rate of growth of output. Population, the labour force, income, and the capital stock are all growing at the same rate. Per capita income is therefore constant, the labour force is always fully employed, and the labour to output ratio and the capital to output ratio can be maintained at the level determined by technology. This is the famous Harrod - Domar condition for equilibrium steady state growth. It is an equilibrium growth path not only in the sense discussed at the beginning of the last paragraph, but also equilibrium in the sense of maintaining full employment and per capita income along the growth path.

If $n > \frac{s}{v}$ we have a situation in which the population and the labour force are growing at a higher rate than that of income and the capital stock. We therefore have both growing unemployment and falling per capita income. The capital stock is not growing fast enough to provide capital for the growing labour force and, because of the assumption of a fixed capital output ratio and therefore a fixed capital labour ratio, the extra labour force is redundant in terms of the production process. If, on the contrary, $n < \frac{s}{v}$ we have a situation in which population and the labour force are growing at a lower rate than the capital stock. Now we can maintain full employment and per capita income but we have redundant capital. The economy is accumulating too much capital relative to the labour force available.

In the above model we have assumed that the factors determining the growth rate of income (s and v), and the growth rate of population (n) were given and fixed over the growth path. It is only by chance, therefore, that they will be related in such a way as to result in an equilibrium steady state growth path. However, the model can easily be developed to take account of varying capital output ratios and saving ratios, and more important to examine how disequilibrium situations will affect these, and under what conditions will the effect be such as to lead to an equilibrium growth rate.[1] The simple model is useful, however, in pointing out the important relationships which determine whether or not we will get an equilibrium growth rate. It emphasizes the importance of the relationship between population growth, certain aspects of technology and certain aspects of saving behaviour.

8.4   Business cycles

Using some of the ideas presented above, we can examine some tentative steps in the direction of a theory of business cycles. Within the model of the economy presented in the first seven chapters of this book we can generate business cycles only with continuous exogenous changes. For example, if for some reason investment expenditures fluctuate this would lead to fluctuations in income, prices, and employment.

[1] For a very lucid elaboration of these questions see R. Solow *Growth Theory*.

However, by incorporating the idea of the accelerator-multiplier relationship developed above, we can get an endogenously determined cycle in the model.

We saw that if investment is a function of the change in income then $\dfrac{\Delta Y}{Y} = \dfrac{s}{v}$. Assume now that we start from a position of less than full employment and income grows at the above rate. As income rises investment rises (the accelerator principle). As investment rises income rises (the multiplier) and so the process continues. Assume now that we reach full employment, and therefore income cannot continue to rise.[1] Will we remain at this level? The answer is no. The accelerator relationship says that for investment to be positive, income has to be *rising*. When the change in income is zero, investment is zero, so that as soon as we reach the full employment level of income, investment falls to zero. However, the fall in investment will, via the multiplier, lead to a fall in income, which via the accelerator will lead to a further fall in investment, and so on. How far can this process continue? When gross investment is zero, net investment is negative and equal to the rate of depreciation. At this point net investment cannot fall any further. As investment stops falling income stops falling (the multiplier). As the change in income becomes zero, net investment becomes zero (the accelerator) and therefore gross investment becomes positive. This leads to a rise in income, and so the process continues.

One point should be stressed. The above discussion of the business cycle, and the previous one on growth, were essentially in terms of arithmetic rather than economics. The assumptions of a given population growth; of given fixed technical coefficients of production; of a given saving ratio, eliminate any problems of choice, ie any economics. The economics and the complications come in when one moves to such questions as what determines saving behaviour? What determines the production techniques chosen? What determines the growth of the labour force? How do these impinge on each other? What forces are generated in disequilibrium and how do these affect behaviour? The development of both growth and business cycle theories has been to answer the above, and similar, questions.

8.5   Inflation

Inflation is a situation of continuously rising prices. In the models of the economy presented previously we can rationalize once and for all changes in the price level but not continuous changes, unless there are continuous exogenous changes either in aggregate demand or supply. We shall first examine possible explanations of inflation within the framework of the comparative static model presented previously. We then

---

[1] This assumption is made for simplicity of exposition only. All that follows could be restated on the assumption that the full employment level of income is itself growing over time, as long as income over the cycle grows at a faster rate than the full employment level of income.

move to more recent developments.

In figure 8.5.1 below we start with an equilibrium situation of less than full employment arising from a fixed money wage of W^o. The equilibrium price level and real income are P_o and Y_o respectively, and there is some level of employment and unemployment associated with that level of real income. Assume now that the government has a policy aim of maintaining 'full employment'. To do this the government carries out some expansionary monetary or fiscal policy. This is shown by the movement of the EE curve to $E'E'$. If this were the end of the story the result of the government policy would be to raise the price level to P', the level of real income to Y', and to lower unemployment by some amount. However, given the fixed money wage and the rise in prices induced by the government policy, there is a fall in the real wage. What if now workers act so as to maintain their real wage? To do that they raise the money wage from W^o to W'. The effect of this is to raise the price level to P'', change the level of income back to Y_o, and the level of unemployment to what it was before

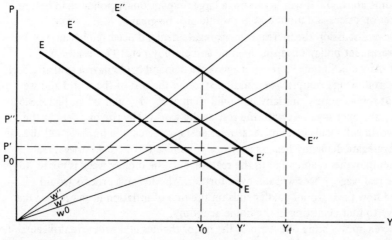

Figure 8.5.1

the introduction of the government policy. Thus the efforts to maintain the real wage have resulted in a rise of the money wage and the price level, with no effect on real income or employment. What if this process continues, ie what if the government continues to maintain its 'full employment' policy and workers continue in their attempt to maintain their real wage? In terms of figure 8.5.1 the EE curve now shifts to $E''E''$ and the money wage to W'', again leaving real income, employment and the real wage unchanged, but raising the money wage and the price level. Of course one does not have to tell the story quite as fast. There may be lags in the adjustment of the money wage to the rise in the price level; and lags in the introduction of the government policies after the appearance of unemployment. Thus unemployment may fall for some time, and so the government policy will be 'successful' until the adjustment in the money wage which will again raise the problem of excessive unemployment.

Let us take this line of analysis a little further. Assume that the process described above has gone on for some time and people begin to expect that prices will continue to rise in the future. At this point, assume we are at Y_0, P_0, and W^0 in figure 8.5.1. Now, as before, the government undertakes some expansionary policy shown by the shift in the EE curve to $E'E'$ and the price level rises to P'. But now, to compensate for the expected price rise in the future, the money wage rate is raised to W''. The adjustment in the money wage, to maintain the real wage, is now made on the basis of the expected price level rather than the current price level. In terms of the current price level this adjustment overcompensates for the rise in prices so the real wage rises and employment and real income fall. Now the government would have to undertake an expansionary policy just to maintain income at Y_0, the level we started off with. To increase income above Y^0 it would require a larger expansionary policy than before, and the effect on prices and money wages would also be greater.

In the above discussion the increases in aggregate demand occurred because of the assumed government policy of raising income and employment. This is clearly unnecessary. Any continuous increase in aggregate demand could have a similar effect. Consider the following example. An inflation starts in the rest of the world and we are looking at some country, initially in equilibrium at P_0, Y_0, and W^0 in figure 8.5.1 which has a fixed exchange rate with the rest of the world. The rise in prices in the rest of the world will result in an increase in exports, a decrease in imports and thus an increase in aggregate demand. This, as previously, will lead to a rise in prices, real income and employment, and a fall in the real wage. If the money wage is raised, to maintain the real wage, prices will rise even further. Whether this process would continue and how far it would go, depends on the rate of inflation in the rest of the world relative to that occurring in the home economy.

The above examples bring out some of the major themes in most current discussions of inflation; expansionary government policy, to achieve certain goals, leading to a rise in prices; adjustment to the rise in prices and, more important, to the expected rise in prices; and the idea of importing inflation from abroad. However, many questions are fudged in the above examples. Why do wages rise even though there is unemployment? What determines the formation of expectations? How fast do people adjust their expectations?

The first step in approaching these questions is to pay more attention to the labour market than we have done until now. When we discussed the labour market in chapter 5 we looked at two possibilities. If money wages are flexible we assumed that there is

a unique full employment equilibrium; if they are rigid there would be some unemployment, depending on the money wage and the price level. In a world in which information,
the changing of acquired skills, and mobility were costless, the assumption of flexible
money wages would lead to the conclusion that there would never by any involuntary
unemployment, ie anybody wanting to work at the going wage rate could do so. He
would find out, at zero cost, where the available job was and what the going wage rate
was; if the skills required were not his he would change them, at zero cost; if the job
was available in a different area he would move, at zero cost. What if all these costs are
not zero? Now we would find that there is always unemployment in a changing
economy. It takes time to find the 'right' job at the 'right' wage; changing patterns of
demand for goods, and changing technology, imply changing demands for particular
skills, and it takes time to learn new ones; it is costly to move and therefore sometimes
worthwhile to wait, even unemployed, in the expectation that mobility will not be
necessary. All the above imply that the concept of full employment is a very ambiguous
one, and not a very sensible one if taken literally to mean that no one is unemployed.

In figure 8.5.2 we represent the labour market by a demand and supply of labour
with respect to the real wage, as before, but as we shall be interested in the behaviour
of the money wage we measure the real wage by a money wage divided by a price level,
which for the moment we assume given. Assume we have flexible money wages. At the
real wage $w_f = \dfrac{W^o}{P^o}$ we have 'full employment' in the sense that there is no excess demand

or supply of labour. However, following the discussion in the previous paragraph, this
does not mean that there is no unemployment. Let us assume that for a given structure
of the labour market the level of unemployment, due to the various causes discussed

above, is u_f. What if the real wage is $w' = \dfrac{W'}{P^o}$? Now we have a situation of an excess

demand for labour and we would expect two things to be true. First, that the level of
unemployment at this real wage is less than u_f. Second, that because of the excess
demand the money wage will rise. The idea behind the first proposition is that if there
is an excess demand for labour all the factors which led to unemployment at 'full
employment' would be mitigated. With an excess demand for labour a wider range of
skills would be demanded, or employers would be willing to substitute available skills
for unavailable but desirable skills; capital would move to areas where labour is
available, thus reducing the cost of mobility to labour, and information would spread
more quickly. We shall therefore assume that there is an indirect relationship between
the level of unemployment and the excess demand for labour.

Given the excess demand for labour, money wages will rise. Until now we assumed
that the wage rate will rise to the equilibrium rate without asking how fast this will
happen or at what rate wages rise, because we were interested in the comparative statics
of the situation. Let us now assume that the rate at which money wages rise also

depends on the excess demand for labour, ie the greater the pressure in the labour market the faster is the rate of change of money wages. We thus have the following two relationships: first, a relationship between the excess demand for labour and the level of unemployment; second, a relationship between the excess demand for labour and the rate of change of money wages. Combining these two we get a relationship

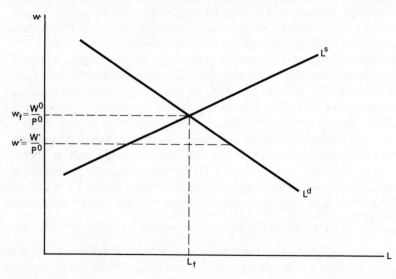

Figure 8.5.2

between the level of unemployment and the rate of change of money wages. We graph such a relationship in figure 8.5.3, where we measure unemployment (u) on the horizontal axis and the percentage change in the money wage rate per period time $(\frac{\dot{W}}{W})$ on the vertical axis. u_f represents the 'full employment' situation, in the sense that there is no tendency for money wages to change, even though there is some unemployment. Any level of unemployment less than u_f implies that money wages will rise because there is an excess demand for labour, and the rate at which they will rise depends on the excess demand for labour, ie the level of unemployment. At any unemployment greater than u_f there is an excess supply of labour and money wages will fall, at a rate depending on the size of the excess supply. The relationship shown in figure 8.5.3 is called the Phillips curve.[1] It was found to hold for the UK for the

[1] It is so called after A.W. Phillips who first discovered the empirical relationship between the change in wages and employment in the UK.

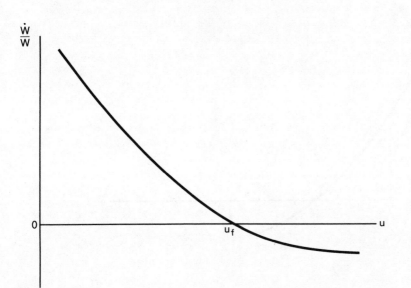

Figure 8.5.3

period 1861 - 1957 with approximately the shape shown in the graph.

So far we have been talking about the relationship between the change in wages and the level of unemployment. What about prices? To relate the above discussion to an analysis of inflation we have to postulate some relationship between a change in money wages and a change in prices. There have been various ways in which this has been done. Mark up theories of pricing postulate that firms raise prices by some given percentage of the change in costs of production. These types of theories are especially prevalent when one is discussing the short run. Other theories, especially when the long run is considered, start from the relationship that the real wage is equal to the marginal product of labour, therefore the change in the real wage will equal the change in the marginal product of labour which occurs because of a changing technology. However, a change in the real wage can be decomposed into a change in the money wage and a change in the price level. Thus, given the change in the marginal product of labour and the change in the money wage, we can derive the change in the price level.[1] For our purpose it does not matter what is the exact relationship between the change in money

---

[1] If m is the marginal product of labour we have $\dfrac{W}{P} = m$ and $\log W - \log P = \log m$

$$\therefore \frac{\dot{W}}{W} - \frac{\dot{P}}{P} = \frac{\dot{m}}{m} \text{ and } \frac{\dot{P}}{P} = \frac{\dot{W}}{W} - \frac{\dot{m}}{m}.$$

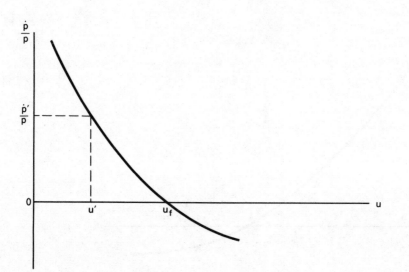

Figure 8.5.4

wages and a change in prices; let us assume however that there is a positive relationship
between the two. We can then translate figure 8.5.3 into figure 8.5.4, where now we
measure the rate of change of prices $\left(\frac{\dot{p}}{p}\right)$ on the vertical axis and unemployment on the
horizontal axis.[1]

Assume now that the government has a policy to maintain the level of unemployment at u', less than u_f. To do that the government has to induce a rate of price change
equal to $\frac{\dot{p}'}{p}$. This relationship has often been used in policy discussions to argue that the
government has a choice between the two desirable goals, no inflation and no unemployment. The government can have no inflation if it is willing to accept the level of
unemployment u_f. This is a more complex development of the first theme discussed
above in terms of our comparative statics model (p. 143) but it does not incorporate
the second theme — expectations and adjustment to them.

Let us again look at the labour market reproduced in figure 8.5.5 below, ignoring

---

[1] This raises a problem we shall ignore. In figure 8.5.2 from which we derive figures 8.5.3 and
8.5.4 we assumed a given price level. Thus a rise in money wages leads to a rise in real wages which
eliminates the excess demand for labour. If now we also have a rise in prices induced by the rise in
money wages the change in the real wage depends on the change in prices also. In the extreme case,
if the rise in prices is equal to the rise in wages nothing happens to real wages and therefore to the
excess demand for labour, and unemployment.

for the moment the dashed curve.

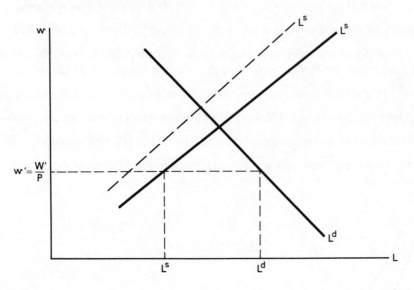

Figure 8.5.5

At the real wage w', the excess demand for labour is $L^d - L^s$ and let us assume that the corresponding level of unemployment is u' in figure 8.5.4 above. In this situation we have rising money wages, and rising prices at a rate of $\dfrac{\dot{p}'}{p}$, a constant real wage and therefore a constant level of unemployment. What if now labour expects prices to continue to rise at this rate? If the expected rise in prices is positive, then for any money wage rate and the current price level, the expected real wage is below the current real wage. If, in deciding how much labour to supply, individuals take account of the expected real wage, then in the above situation the supply curve for labour for any current real wage will be to the left of the one shown. Let the dashed supply curve in figure 8.5.5 be such a supply curve for a positive expected change in the price level and therefore an expected real wage lower than the current real wage. We can see that the excess demand for labour at the real wage w' is greater once the expectations of a rising price level are incorporated. Given a greater excess demand for labour the change in the money wage will be greater than before, and translating this to the Phillips curve (figure 8.5.3), the curve would move to the right, ie we would get a different curve for the case when the expected change in the price level is positive than for that when the expected change is zero. By a similar argument we could get many different Phillips curves for different expectations about the change in the price level. The greater is the expected change in the price level the further to the right would the curve be.

Assume now that the government, via policy, achieves the level of unemployment u' in figure 8.5.6 with prices rising at the rate $\frac{\dot{p}'}{p}$. Now, individuals start expecting this rate of change of prices. As soon as this happens the whole curve shifts out to the dashed one which represents the Phillips curve when the expected change in the price level is equal to $\frac{\dot{p}'}{p}$. Thus we may have a situation where instead of trading more inflation for less unemployment we have more inflation and the same amount of unemployment. Now to achieve the level of unemployment u' the necessary rate of inflation becomes $\frac{\dot{p}''}{p}$. As soon as this becomes expected there will be another shift of the curve and we are back where we started.

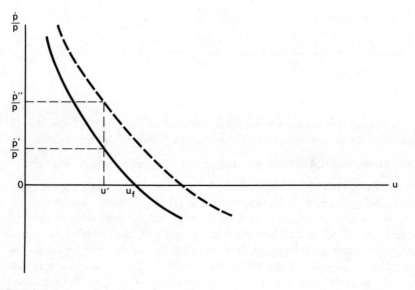

Figure 8.5.6

In the above discussion of inflation we have skimmed over many important issues which are at the centre of the current theoretical controversies about inflation and unemployment. To cite but a few; how fast are expectations about inflation formed, and how important are such expectations to current decisions about the supply of labour? How do employers incorporate inflation and expectations about inflation into their decisions? What repercussion does the rate of inflation have on the money sector and the expectations of inflation on interest rates? What are the costs of both inflation and unemployment? What are the costs of stopping inflation once expectations about it have been formed? To answer these questions another book is necessary. Hopefully, the curious will read one and the inspired write one.

references

1 *Consumption*
DUESENBERRY J S 'Income-Consumption Relations and Their Implications' in
    M G Mueller (ed.) *Readings in Macroeconomics* Holt, Rinehart and Winston 1966.
EVANS Michael K *Macroeconomic Activity* Harper International Edition 1969.
    Chapters 2 and 3.
FARRELL M J 'The New Theories of the Consumption Function' *Economic Journal*
    December 1959.
FRIEDMAN M *A Theory of the Consumption Function* Princeton University
    Press 1957.

2 *Investment*
KNOX A D 'The Acceleration Principle and the Theory of Investment: A Survey'
    Economica August 1952.
WHITE W H 'Interest Elasticity of Investment Demand' *American Economic Review*
    September 1956.

3 *Growth and Cycles*
ALLEN R G D *Macro-Economic Theory* Macmillan 1967.
    Chapters 10 - 12.
HAHN F H and MATHEWS R C O 'The Theory of Economic Growth', *Economic
    Journal* December 1964.
JOHNSON H G *Essays in Monetary Economics* George Allen and Unwin 1967.
    Chapter 4.
MATHEWS R C O *The Trade Cycle* Cambridge University Press 1959.
SOLOW R M *Growth Theory an Exposition* Oxford University Press 1970.

4 *Inflation*
BRONFENBRENNER M and HOLZMAN F D 'Survey of Inflation Theory' *American
    Economic Review* October 1963.
FRIEDMAN M 'The Role of Monetary Policy' *American Economic Review* March 1968.

JOHNSON H G *Essays in Monetary Economics* George Allen and Unwin 1967. Chapter 3.

LIPSEY R G 'The Relation Between Unemployment and the Rate of Change of Money Wages in the United Kingdom, 1862 - 1957: A Further Analysis' *Economica* February 1960.

REES A 'The Phillips Curve as a Menu for Policy Choices' *Economica* August 1970.

questions

chapter 2

1 'The equilibrium level of real income necessarily requires equality between intended investment and intended saving.'

'The equilibrium level of real income necessarily requires equality between aggregate demand and aggregate supply.'

What is the relationship between the above two statements?

2 What is held constant along the IS curve? What does this mean?

3 If all prices change, will this lead to a shift in the IS curve? What behavioural assumption is crucial to your answer?

4 Assume the consumption function is of the form $C=f(Y, \frac{M}{P})$ where $\frac{M}{P}$ is the real quantity of money. Answer question 3.

5 Assume that investment also depends on the level of real income, say, $I=g_0 -g_1 r+g_2 Y$ and consumption, as in the text, is $C= a+bY$. What is the value of the multiplier? Derive the IS curve for this case. Will the slope of this IS curve be steeper or flatter than that of the one derived on the assumption in the text that $I= g_0 -g_1 r$? What is the economic explanation for the difference in the slopes?

6 In the chapter we assume that (a) $C=f(Y)$ (real consumption depends on real income). Consider the following two alternative assumptions; (b) $PC=f(Y)$ (the money value of consumptions depends on real income), and (c) $C=f(PY)$ (real consumption depends on money income).

(i)   Would the condition for equilibrium in the goods sector be affected if we assume (b) or (c)?

(ii)   Answer question 3 assuming first (b) and then (c).

(iii)   Assume that the level of output is fixed at Y and investment at I. If desired expenditures are greater than the level of output, prices (P) rise; if output is greater than desired expenditures, prices fall. Can this force, the change in prices, solve a disequilibrium situation? Answer for the assumptions about consumption represented by (a), (b) and (c) above.

chapter 3

1 What is held constant along the LM curve?

2 Assume that from some initial equilibrium situation people lose confidence in the banks and decide to hold more currency rather than deposits. What will happen to the LM curve?

3 Analyse the following quotations (a) 'It is nonsense to suggest that banks can create money. A banker can only lend money deposited with him. For it to be deposited it must already exist.' (b) 'Every bank loan creates a bank deposit which becomes the basis of another loan. The banks have thus played a major part in the process of money creation.'

4 Assume credit cards become generally acceptable and people use them partly as a substitute for money. How would that affect the LM curve? What if they become generally acceptable but only as a substitute for currency?

5 Everybody suddenly expects that an inflation will occur. What will happen to the demand for money and the LM curve if: (a) the only assets in which wealth can be held are money and bonds? (b) wealth can be held in the form of money, bonds and houses? In case (b) what will happen to the price of houses?

chapter 4

1 In the simple IS - LM model presented in this chapter, will a change in real income lead to a shift in the IS curve, the LM curve, or both? Why is this a nonsense question?

2 Assume that investment does not depend on the interest rate. This implies that the IS curve is perfectly inelastic (why?). Will changes in the quantity of money affect real income or the interest rate? Will changes in the price level affect real income or the interest rate? What if the consumption function is of the form $C=f(Y,\frac{M}{P})$?

3 Construct an IS - LM model in which you assume that investment does not depend on the interest rate, and the demand for money does not depend on income. In that model what determines real income? What determines the interest rate?

4 Somebody tells you that the value of the multiplier ($\frac{1}{1-b}$) is 3, and asks you to predict the effect on real income of an increase in desired expenditures of 100. What other information would you want? How would you use it?

5 What is the effect on real income and the interest rate of the following:
(a) Because of a change in expectations people want to invest more at all interest rates.
(b) Because of a change in expectations people want to hold more money at all interest rates.
(c) Because of a spate of payroll robberies all wages are paid by cheque rather than cash.

(d) Because of a spate of bank robberies people lose confidence in the banks and convert their deposits into currency.

(e) Because a new tax is to be introduced people buy consumer durables in the current period. What will happen to real income both in the current period and in the next period?

6 Analyse the following quotation: 'If people desire to save more there will be an increase in the demand for financial assets, for example bonds, and therefore a fall in the interest rate. The fall in the interest rate will lead to a rise in investment and thus, via the multiplier, a rise in income. In this way an increase in saving leads to a rise in income.'

chapter 5

1 Are the following two statements correct for an economy with flexible wages and prices in full employment equilibrium.

(a) If everybody decides to save more (a shift of the saving function) investment will rise.

(b) If everybody decides to invest more (a shift in the investment function) investment will remain unchanged.

2 Discuss the following: 'The simple multiplier is equal to $\frac{1}{1-b}$. However this over-states the effect on income of a change in desired expenditures because of:

(a) repercussions via the interest rate

(b) repercussions via the price level.'

Can (b) be operative if (a) is not?

3 Assume an economy with a fixed money wage in equilibrium at less than full employment. What are the effects on real income, the price level and the interest rate if

(a) a cut in money wages

(b) an increase in the quantity of money

(c) a cut in taxes.

4 How would you analyze the following fictitious (but not far fetched) election manifesto: 'When we get into office we shall make sure that the interest rate is low – so that investment and the rate of growth will be high. We shall increase the building of hospitals and schools. And last but not least we shall make sure that consumption continues to grow at a rate we have all come to expect. Moreover, we promise to achieve all this while keeping down the rate of inflation.'

5 Assuming an economy with flexible wages and prices. Examine the effects on real income, the real wage rate, the interest rate and the price level of:

(a) A technological innovation which makes it possible to get a higher level of output with the use of the same quantity of inputs, but leaves the marginal product of labour unchanged.

(b)   A technological innovation as in (a) but one which also increases the marginal product of labour.

(c)   A change in tastes such that people now prefer more leisure relative to goods.

6   Answer question (5) assuming an economy with a fixed money wage at less than full employment equilibrium.

chapter 6

1   Assume an economy is in equilibrium. The government now raises taxes and uses the proceeds to reduce its outstanding debt (i.e. it buys back government bonds). What effect will this have on real income, the price level and the rate of interest?

2   In a situation of less than full employment the government increase old age pensions and employment benefits. It finances this by raising taxes by an equal amount. What effect will this have on real income?

3   In a situation of less than full employment the government increases expenditures on hospitals and schools. It finances this by raising taxes by an equal amount. What effect will this have on real income? Compare the answer to this question with that to question 2 above. Explain the differences. (If your answers are the same, try again)

4   Assume that real income fluctuates over time because of fluctuations in investment. The government now introduces the following rule: one part of government expenditures, G_0, will be undertaken whatever the level of real income. Another part, G_1, will be positively related to real income, say $G_1 = \alpha Y$. Will this rule lead to a reduction in the fluctuation of real income?

5   An economy is in equilibrium at less than full employment with a fixed money wage of W_0. The government wants to increase the level of real income and reduce the price level. It can use monetary policy, fiscal policy, an incomes policy or some combination of the three. What policy or policies would you recommend?

6   Because of a war a government has to increase its expenditures on goods and services. It can finance this either by increasing taxes, borrowing, or printing money. Which method of financing would you recommend? Consider the effects of the financing both in the current period ('during the war') and in the future ('after the war').

chapter 7

1   Are the following two statements correct for an economy with flexible wages and prices:

(a)   If exports rise investment will fall

(b)   If imports rise investment will rise.

2   After the British devaluation the government tightened monetary policy and increased taxes. The purpose of these policies was 'to make devaluation work'.

Why are such policies necessary and how would they achieve their aim?

3   Country A maintains a fixed exchange rate. It is at full employment and has a severe balance of payments deficit. Discuss the merits of each of the following policy changes:

(a)   Devaluation

(b)   A decrease in the stock of money

(c)   A decrease in the budget deficit.

4   An economy with a fixed money wage is in equilibrium at less than full employment. It now receives, as a gift, goods and services from the rest of the world. What effect will this have on output, the rate of interest, the price level and the real wage rate?

5   An economy is in equilibrium at less than full employment. What effect will the following have on real income, the price level and the balance of payments?

(a)   A long dock strike reduces exports

(b)   The rate of inflation in the rest of the world increases

(c)   The rest of the world raises tariffs

(d)   The government increases foreign aid in the form of goods and services given, as a gift, to other countries.

chapter 8

1   The government raises taxes. At the same time it promises that next year it will cut taxes back to the original level. What effect will this have on real income, assuming

(a)   the relative income hypothesis of consumption?

(b)   the permanent income hypothesis of consumption?

2   Assume that everybody expects the same rate of inflation? Because of this all wage contracts include a price index clause, i.e. the money wage rate is to rise at the same rate as the price level. How would this change the Phillips curve analysis of inflation?

3   Can a country on a flexible exchange rate 'import' inflation from abroad?

4   It has been said that if everybody expects an inflation to continue it is very difficult or costly to stop the inflation. Why is it more difficult to stop an inflation which is expected to continue, than one which is not expected to continue?

index